JESUS REDISCOVERED: THOUGHTS ON LIFE IN JESUS CHRIST

Joshua Benjamin

Cover design by David Ramirez.
www.davidramirezdesign.com

First Printing: 2014

ISBN-13: 978-1494476496
ISBN-10: 1494476495

For Lambert

CONTENTS

CHAPTER 01 – AN ABUNDANT LIFE IN CHRIST

"I came that they may have life and have it abundantly." (John 10:10)

Jesus. This book, like any worthwhile work of literature, must begin with Him. In fact, the whole of this book must be about Him. Every letter sprawled across every page must point to Jesus, or else they'll be mere empty marks—thick black letters on vacant white pages. Christ is the one thing of eternal value a preacher can share from the pulpit, singular in majesty and unmatched in worth. It is of great benefit that this is made clear from the outset. I can offer you nothing of genuine worth except for Him. And so this book has been written to that end.

Jesus Christ proclaimed in the Gospel of John that He "came that they might have life and have it abundantly" (John 10:10). This promise of abundant life is pledged to all of Christ's sheep—every believer that has responded to the gospel by repenting of their sins and placing their faith in Him alone for salvation. And yet as

1

I've read and meditated on these words countless times, I've caught myself wondering: Why is there so little depth in spiritual life displayed in the church today? Why do so many of Christ's sheep appear starved and anemic?

The more I have considered this, the more I am convinced of the answer: *Christians aren't looking for life in the right place.* While many church leaders continue to peddle flashy programs, weekend conferences, Christian diet fads, and best-selling books, they fail to recognize that spiritual life itself is not found in any of these things. Life is not found in a *thing*, but rather it is found in a Person. Jesus gives life. "*I* came," He declares, "That they might have life and have it abundantly." One can sift through a library of books, attend endless Christian conferences, and spend a lifetime planted in a dusty pew, but if Jesus Christ isn't the center of any of those things, they are empty. They will be spiritually barren. So when we speak of such wonderful topics such as justification, righteousness, sanctification, and eternal life, we must understand them within the context of a mighty Savior who died and rose from the dead, for spiritual life is not found apart from Jesus Christ.

When Jesus spoke the words, "I came that they may have life and have it abundantly," He spoke them in *contrast* to the thief—the devil—who came "only to steal and kill and destroy." (John 10:10). The thief is very cunning. He has many avenues to destruction. The thief steals and destroys not just through heartache and suffering, but also through pleasure, distraction, and unceasing entertainment. Sadly, often what is mere entertainment is passed off today as beneficial and even spiritual. Walk into any Christian bookstore. There is an avalanche of books on the shelves, but too many of them lack spiritual depth or reality. I remember a few years ago speaking with a friend who held in his hands a book which at that time was a Christian best-seller. I asked him about it.

"This book is terrific," he remarked, "It's really changing my life."

"Really? What's it about?"

"Oh, I don't know. I can't quite explain. The author tells a bunch of stories about his friends and himself." How absurd, I thought. This young man (who was very sincere in his faith) was excited about a book that he believed was changing his life, and he couldn't even tell me anything about it. I decided to read the book myself. It was well-written and wildly entertaining, but like so many things offered today, it had little spiritual value. Where was Jesus in all of this? The book barely even mentioned Him, nor was the gospel discussed. Was this the abundant life Christ so dearly promised? I knew my time had been robbed from me. And yet I felt this book typifies what is offered to Christians as spiritual "food." The thief has many devices to steal and kill and destroy, even from within the sheepfold.

Why must so much of what is offered in churches today be so cheap and easy? When did Christian spirituality go the way of fast-food marketing and vending machine conveniences? The books we read and the church programs that are pushed onto Christians today are only as worthwhile as much as they point us to *Him* ("...in Him was life" John 1:4). It is always Jesus Christ that gives life. We must keep this distinction in our minds as we search the Scriptures and explore the deep spiritual life that is every Christian's birthright in Jesus. Likewise, we must not fool ourselves; no mere book in itself can change a life, not even this one. But my sincere prayer is that this book will point you down a path towards deeper intimacy with the one person who has transformed lives for the past two-thousand years: Jesus Christ.

SEEKING GOD

While the apostle Paul was in Athens his spirit was provoked inside him, for the city was full of idols (Acts 17:16). As he passed through the streets he began to preach Jesus and the resurrection. Yet no one understood him, so they brought the apostle to Mars Hill—the place in the city where the men would gather to discuss and listen to new ideas. As Paul stood in their midst, he began to preach to them the things that they were ignorant of, that God who created the heavens and earth did not dwell in temples made by human hands (Acts 17:24). He explained that the Lord created from Adam all nations and peoples, and has determined where and when they dwell for one reason: "That they should seek God, in hope that they might feel their way toward him and find him. Yet he is actually not far from each one of us" (Acts 17:27).

He created us that we might seek Him. The Lord of all glory desires for each of us to reach out to Him and find Him and know Him. *And yet He is not far from each one of us.* The constant joy of my life has been seeking God, and knowing Him, and Jesus Christ whom He sent. In times of hardship and struggle, I've found that He is very close indeed, closer than I know, and that Christ's presence would be near to me if I would just draw near to

Him (James 4:8).

And yet not everyone seeks Him. The Scriptures teach that no sinner seeks after God (Romans 3:10-18). Only after the Spirit has changed the heart of the sinner do they search for Him. After God has captured our affections, *then* the real hunt has begun. David writes in a psalm, "You have said, 'Seek my face.' My heart says to you, 'Your face, Lord, do I seek'" (Psalm 27:8). *Has He put it in your heart to seek Him?*

There is one thing that is of first importance: "That Christ died for our sins in accordance with the Scriptures, that he was buried, that he was raised on the third day in accordance with the Scriptures" (1 Corinthians 15:3-4). It is because of *this* historical fact—that Jesus Christ died for our sins and rose from the dead—that we are able to seek and find God. And because He rose from the dead, we know Jesus will return again to judge the world in righteousness. The apostle Paul pleaded with the men of Athens:

> "The times of ignorance God overlooked, but now he commands all people everywhere to repent, because he has fixed a day on which he will judge the world in righteousness by a man whom he has appointed; and of this he has given assurance to all by raising him from the dead." (Acts 17:30-31)

Christ rose from the dead and is coming again. He calls everyone to repent of their sins and to trust in Him for salvation. "If you confess with your mouth that Jesus is

Lord and believe in your heart that God raised him from the dead, you will be saved" (Romans 10:9). To those who reject Jesus is eternal condemnation. To those who receive Him is eternal life. If you haven't already given yourself to Jesus Christ, will you seek Him now?

I have often struggled in my soul's quest to seek God. I strain to figure out what a life that pursues the Lord should look like today. I do not always have the answer. However, Scripture does give a few clues:

> And without faith it is impossible to please him, for whoever would draw near to God must believe that he exists and that he rewards those who seek him. (Hebrews 11:6)

God rewards those who seek Him. He does not reward us financially, He does not guarantee us a life of wealth and ease, nor does He promise that we won't suffer or face trials and tribulation. What we receive instead, however, is a life of grace and truth, even at times in spite of our situations. The Lord rewards us with Himself, and with His presence (Lamentations 3:25, Psalm 16:11). And knowing God in Christ is the difference between life and death: "And this is eternal life, that they know you the only true God, and Jesus Christ whom you have sent" (John 17:3).

Seeking God requires diligence. God spoke through the prophet Jeremiah, "You will seek me and find me. When you seek me with all your heart, I will be found by you, declares the Lord" (Jeremiah 29:13-14). We must be patient in our pursuit of God. Jesus invites us to sit at His feet, to rest, to learn from Him and grow in Him. These things take time. There is no formula for quick spiritual maturity; it is a lifelong task of discipline and sacrifice to pursue Him. The Lord spent 40 years in the wilderness preparing the Israelites to enter the land He promised to Abraham. And so it is in our faith. This is a call for patience and discipline, for those who seek God diligently are the ones He rewards.

Do you desire to seek God? That is why He created you and placed you where you are now. Seek Him with all your heart, soul, and might. Jesus once spoke to His disciples, explaining, "The kingdom of heaven has suffered violence, and the violent take it by force" (Matthew 11:12). Those who show little zeal in their faith do not find Him. We must become as men of violence, pressing into the kingdom, sacrificing all to seek after the Lord. Our reward is found in Jesus, who promises life abundantly. *Will you seek Him?*

WHOEVER HAS THE SON HAS LIFE

The apostle John wrote in one of his letters:

> And this is the testimony, that God gave us eternal life, and this life is in his Son. Whoever has the Son has life; whoever does not have the Son of God does not have life. (1 John 5:11-12)

Is it really that black-and-white? Whoever has the Jesus Christ has life, and whoever does not have Him does not have life? This is what the Scriptures declare. Eternal life is found only in the Son of God. Apart from the Him there is no life, only shadows. Eternal life and the abundant life that Christ proclaimed are terms that go together. "Abundant" describes the *quality* of life we experience in Christ, while "eternal" speaks of the *quantity* of this life—one that stretches on forever, into eternity. It is a life that that is born at the moment of faith and never ends. As we shall explore later, eternal life, as well as abundant life, means we are partakers of the divine nature. These two ideas form a beautiful whole and describe the life that is found in Jesus Christ.

What does abundant life look like? First, it is a life overflowing with the love of Jesus. It has a joy that is greater than any other. Abundant life in Christ is characterized by true holiness and heartfelt obedience to God's law. It is a life of such tangible peace that it surpasses all understanding. It is the kind of life described by the apostle Paul in his letter to the Galatians, when he explained the fruit of the Spirit: "But the fruit of the Spirit is love, joy, peace, patience, kindness, goodness, faithfulness, gentleness, self-control; against such things there is no law" (Galatians 5:22-23). And most importantly, abundant life is the mark of true spirituality and is lived in an intimate fellowship with the Savior. *Abundant life is readily available to all of Christ's sheep.*

And yet for many Christians there is something missing. There are Christians who have Jesus—"*Whoever has the Son has life*"—and yet don't experience a vibrant spiritual life. These are the ones whom are crushed, driven to despair, and feel forsaken and even destroyed. Many Christians do not sense God's presence or His joy within, but instead are just barely getting by, as if they are treading water spiritually. I am convinced that often the problem with many Christians is that their faith lacks content and authenticity. Not only do they not know *how* to live out the basic tenets of their faith, they often don't even know basic Christian doctrine. There is a dismal disconnect in their faith.

This problem is not due to a lack of church programs. Of course there are plenty of church meetings, and Bible studies, and books to read. Yet one of the great tragedies in the modern church, however, is that the programs often don't work, or else they only have a very gilded effect. I'm convinced that this failure stems from too many of these activities being done simply as an end to themselves. People foolishly believe that if they would simply read a book or attend some flashy conference or find the right small group, then their lives would finally be transformed. They would find the spiritual reality that they feel they are missing. Yet this isn't quite true. Things don't transform lives; God transforms lives. He changes people through the gospel, the finished work of Jesus Christ, along with the empowering presence of the Holy Spirit. *It is only in the person of Jesus Christ that we find the ultimate reality, the answer to the most fundamental needs of the human condition.* If the meetings we attend or books we read lead us to the risen Christ, then we will be changed. If they don't, we'll inevitably remain the same.

This tendency to misuse the otherwise good things that the Lord has gifted has plagued the people of God for ages. I have in my mind now an illustration from the Old Testament, when the nation of Israel was wandering in the wilderness. The people became impatient, and they spoke out against God and against Moses. So God punished them by sending fiery serpents to bite the rebellious people, and many Israelites died. What God also did, however, was provide a means of salvation:

> And the Lord said to Moses, "Make a serpent and set it on a pole, and everyone who is bitten, when he sees it, shall live." So Moses made a bronze serpent and set it on a pole. And if a serpent bit anyone, he would look at the bronze serpent and live. (Numbers 21:8-9)

God instructed Moses to make a serpent of bronze. If anyone was bitten by a serpent, all they would need to do was to look away to the bronze serpent and they would live. God had given his people the bronze serpent as a means of deliverance. Sadly, years later many Israelites turned this same bronze serpent into an object of worship. They had taken a good thing that God had given them and turned it into an idol. So Hezekiah—who was king of Israel at that time—destroyed the serpent.

> He removed the high places and broke the pillars and cut down the Asherah. And he broke in pieces the bronze serpent that Moses had made, for until those days the people of Israel had made offerings to it (it was called Nehushtan). (2 Kings 18:4)

Hezekiah exposed the serpent as it really was—a thing of

brass. There was no power or reality in the object itself. Truly the reality was in what the serpent pointed to— mercy and salvation offered by the Lord. Christ later explained that the true message of the brass serpent pointed to his future death on the cross. "And as Moses lifted up the serpent in the wilderness, so must the Son of Man be lifted up, that whoever believes in him may have eternal life" (John 3:14-15). We must not fail to learn the lesson of the brass serpent. We must look past the objects and the programs towards a mighty Savior who offers grace, reality, and life. "Whoever has the Son has life; whoever does not have the Son does not have life" (1 John 5:12). We must remain focused and seek Jesus Christ in the midst of the noise and distractions that the modern church has created.

JESUS CHRIST: THE BREAD OF LIFE

It is very common for people to remain blind to the spiritual reality in front of them, even during the days of Christ. I am thinking now of the time when Jesus fed the multitude in John's gospel. The crowd that was with Him in that desolate place was starving and yet had nothing to eat. So Jesus broke five barley loaves and two fishes, and was able to perform a stunning miracle and feed a multitude that numbered over five-thousand men. The people responded with predictable fervor:

> When the people saw the sign that he had done, they said, "This is indeed the Prophet who is to come into the world!"

> Perceiving then that they were about to
> come and take him by force to make him
> king, Jesus withdrew again to the
> mountain by himself. (John 6:14-15).

The crowd was going to take Jesus by force and crown
Him as their king, but Christ was able to sneak away. The
next day, after they realized that He had left, the people
began to search for Jesus. Now this wasn't a half-hearted
seeking. They climbed into boats and sailed across the Sea
of Galilee—all the way to Capernaum—just to find Jesus.
After all that effort to see the Messiah, you would imagine
that Jesus would praise them for their faith. But Christ
knew the truth! He knew what was in the heart of man:

> When they found him on the other side
> of the sea, they said to him, "Rabbi, when
> did you come here?" Jesus answered
> them, "Truly, truly, I say to you, you are
> seeking me, not because you saw signs,
> but because you ate your fill of the loaves.
> Do not labor for the food that perishes,
> but for the food that endures to eternal
> life, which the Son of Man will give you.
> For on him God the Father has set his
> seal." Then they said to him, "What must
> we do, to be doing the works of God?"
> Jesus answered them, "This is the work of
> God, that you believe in him whom he
> has sent." (John 6:25-29)

The crowd only sought Christ because He had fed them a

day before. They were following Jesus, *not* because of who He *was*, but because of what He had done for them. Even after witnessing Christ's miracle and the fanaticism with which the crowd responded, they still failed to grasp the deeper reality that Jesus was trying to show them. What was their mistake? *The people could not look past the types and shadows and see the spiritual reality.* They sought the benefit of knowing Christ, but did not seek Christ Himself. They had tasted the broken barley loaves and fishes; they had even rightly connected Christ's miracle with Moses providing manna for the Israelites in the wildness. Yet they failed to grasp what these signs meant, or the spiritual reality that these miracles pointed to. Christ tried to open their eyes:

> Jesus then said to them, "Truly, truly, I say to you, it was not Moses who gave you the bread from heaven, but my Father gives you the true bread from heaven. For the bread of God is he who comes down from heaven and gives life to the world." They said to him, "Sir, give us this bread always." Jesus said to them. "I am the bread of life; whoever comes to me shall not hunger, and whoever believes in me shall never thirst." (John 6:32-35)

At first the crowd wanted this bread—"Sir, give us this bread always." However, once Christ explained to them what this bread meant—what believing and knowing Jesus Christ *really* is like—they complained that His words were

13

much too demanding. In the end they abandoned Jesus and would have nothing to do with Him. Christ had explained to them that believing in Him was like eating His flesh and drinking His blood:

> So Jesus said to them, "Truly, truly, I say to you, unless you eat the flesh of the Son of Man and drink his blood, you have no life in you. Whoever feeds on my flesh and drinks my blood has eternal life, and I will raise him up on the last day. For my flesh is true food, and my blood is true drink. Whoever feeds on my flesh and drinks my blood abides in me, and I in him. As the living Father sent me, and I live because of the Father, so whoever feeds on me, he will live because of me. This is the bread that came down from heaven, not as the fathers ate and died. Whoever feeds on this bread will live forever." (John 6:53-58)

This is the lesson of the True Bread that has come down from heaven: Following Christ is not a little thing; it is a deep, deep thing. Knowing Jesus and having a relationship with Him are not cheap clichés, as it is so often reduced to in the modern church. They are a deep and intimate reality. It is as eating His flesh and drinking His blood. And we can learn from this. Do you come to Christ and believe in Christ? Jesus stands in our midst and shouts, "Come to Me! Rest in Me! Believe in Me! Find all of your satisfaction, hopes, dreams, joy, salvation, life, everything in Me!" And yet we don't come. So often, whenever we have a problem or begin to realize that *something* is missing at the core of our faith—a reality that is not so much a thing, but rather a Person (for the apostle Paul cried out, "*Who* will deliver me from this body of death?" rather than "*What* will deliver me.")—we sadly reach for a *thing* to try to fill our need. We labor for food that perishes. We might pick up a devotional or some other book, or to go on a weekend retreat, or sign up for a short term mission trip, or even find a different church group to fill this missing reality. Yet if these things are done *as an end to themselves*, apart from the person of Jesus Christ, they will ultimately be worthless. Everyone in the wilderness who ate of the manna eventually died, but the person who eats of Jesus Christ will live forever. Likewise, the person who feeds upon Christ daily will find the deepest needs of the human heart met in the Him. Bread speaks of nourishment and satisfaction. The Christian who satisfies themselves on Jesus will thrive in their faith. *They will possess life.* Every spiritual endeavor outside of the person of Christ is dead. Even the loaves that Jesus fed the multitude only satisfied them for a single day. And yet there is the True Bread— the life of Jesus Christ—that will satisfy always: "I am the bread of life; whoever comes to me shall not hunger, and whoever believes in me shall never thirst" (John 6:35).

If we understand Christ's words in the Gospel of John, we can see how challenging His teaching really is. It is a radical call to walk by faith and to look to Jesus Christ for life. Tell me, what are you doing to *not* labor for the bread that perishes? Having you been searching for something real, but in the end only have been grasping after shadows? Our eyes must be open to see Jesus. Many people turned away from Christ because of how difficult they found His words to be. We must become like Simon Peter, who spoke up after Jesus asked if the disciples wanted to abandon Him as well: "Simon Peter answered him, 'Lord to whom shall we go? You have the words of eternal life, and we have believed, and have come to know, that you are the Holy One of God'" (John 6:68-69). Only Jesus Christ has the words of eternal life. We must learn to keep church programs, books, and everything else in their rightful place—as things that should ultimately draw us closer to Him, that *He* might give us life. *Will you look to Jesus for life?*

ALL THINGS THAT PERTAIN TO LIFE AND GODLINESS

The apostle Peter writes:

> His divine power has granted to us all things that pertain to life and godliness, through the knowledge of him who called us to his own glory and excellence, by which he has granted to us his precious and very great promises, so that through them you may become partakers of the divine nature, having escaped the corruption that is in the world because of sinful desire. (2 Peter 1:3-4)

Every Christian has been given everything in Christ that they will ever need for life and godliness. This means that every believer, without exception, has everything needed to

ual life in Jesus Christ. There is no
-rate Christian. How can Peter say
e have become "partakers of the
possess all things. *Because we are in*
hrist is in us, we possess every spiritual
"Blessed by the God and Father of
st, who has blessed us in Christ with
ing in the heavenly places" (Ephesians
ystical and spiritual union with Christ,
dden all the treasures of wisdom and
knowledge" (Colossians 2:3). Christ is our all in all. He
meets our deepest needs as human beings. He is the
eternal Word of God, the very agent of creation. "For by
him all things were created, in heaven and on earth, visible
and invisible, whether thrones or dominions or rulers or
authorities—all things were created through him and for
him" (Colossians 1:16). This means that both the physical
and spiritual were created by Jesus and find their ultimate
purpose in Him. And in Christ we possess every spiritual
blessing.

After Peter explains that Christians have been given
everything they need pertaining to life and godliness, he
then gives clear instructions of our responsibilities from
becoming "partakers of the divine nature:"

> For this very reason, make every effort to
> supplement your faith with virtue, and
> virtue with knowledge, and knowledge
> with self-control, and self-control with
> steadfastness, and steadfastness with
> godliness, and godliness with brotherly
> affection, and brotherly affection with

love. (2 Peter 1:5-7)

These are seven qualities with which our faith should be supplemented with: Virtue, knowledge, self-control, steadfastness, godliness, brotherly affection, and love. And then what are we told? "For if these qualities are yours and are increasing, they keep you from being ineffective or unfruitful in the knowledge of our Lord Jesus Christ" (2 Peter 1:8). What we discover from this passage is this: *It is quite possible to have a very high knowledge of God and yet remain barren and unfruitful.* This epidemic is exactly what is plaguing so much of the modern church. There are Christians who are ineffective and unfruitful in their faith. They lack power and reality. And there is no amount of self-effort that they can muster to find deliverance. Consequently, many Christians turn to other *things* to find what is missing in their lives, instead of looking away to the divine life that has been imparted to them—the life of Jesus Christ, who has made His home within the heart of every Christian.

THE TRUTH WILL SET YOU FREE

Even Bible study, done as an end to itself, comes with a warning. Do not misunderstand: The Bible is the inerrant, inspired Word of God. Christians should take seriously their study of Scripture. However, merely gaining Biblical knowledge, knowledge to puff up inside of us, may have little spiritual value—if not given its proper place.

Christ taught His disciples, "If you abide in my word, you are truly my disciples, and you will know the truth, and the truth will set you free" (John 8:31-32). Over the last few years I have often turned these words over in my mind—"the truth will set you free." If you know truth, it will set you free. It seems so simple, right? Yet as wonderful as the promise of freedom is, I've discovered an overarching experience in my life: Many times I know a truth, but I don't have any freedom. Did Jesus make a mistake in what He said? Of course not! There's a crucial distinction that must be understood to see *how* the truth sets us free.

Jesus said that knowing God's truth will set us free. But just a few words later, He *clarified* what He meant: "…if the Son sets you free, you will be free indeed" (John 8:36). This is the key to freedom. It is only by taking the truths in Scripture and connecting them with Jesus Christ that we will experience true liberty. We must never forget that Scripture ultimately points to an infinite, personal God who is present and offers life. This God became flesh in Jesus Christ. His words cannot be reduced into mere abstractions. Biblical truth goes hand-in-hand with a living God who is near and delights in setting captives free. Jesus proclaimed Himself to be "the way, the truth, and the life" (John 14:6). When He says, "I am the way," He means there is no way outside of Him. Or says, "I am the truth," He means that He Himself *is* truth. Or, "I am the life," that there is *no* life outside of Him. The Christian life must *always* be lived within the context of a relationship with Jesus. Any truth we learn must ultimately find its place in Him. Biblical truth, apart from the living person of Christ, will almost always lead to sterile doctrine or lifeless dogma.

Christ once rebuked the Pharisees, saying, "You

search the Scriptures because you think that in them you have eternal life; and it is they that bear witness about me, yet you refuse to come to me that you may have life" (John 5:39-40). These words are of great importance, because here is a sad and common tragedy: It easy for even sincere Christians to study the Bible and yet remained unchanged. One man may read the Scriptures and find the sweetest transforming grace, and begin to pursue the deepest depths of spiritual reality. The next man can read the same words, close his Bible, and go about his business as if nothing happened. What is the difference? The first fellow searched the Scriptures, and then came to Jesus for life. The second did not. The first man took the words he read and sought out the Savior those words pointed to. The next man refused to come to Christ for life. Either experience could be ours. Our eyes must be opened to see Jesus. If we fail to connect the individual truths we read in the Bible with Him, we risk falling short of the freedom that Jesus promised. Would you like to be free *indeed?* Freedom will only come in the one who is truth Himself— Jesus Christ. We must be diligent to take the truths we find in the Bible and apply them within relationship to the Savior.

Our faithful Rabbi, Jesus Christ, eagerly invites us to come to Him, and learn from Him, and to take His yoke upon ourselves (Matthew 11:28). Wrestle with Jesus as you meditate upon His words. Spend time in His presence, asking him what these words mean. The Scriptures bear witness about Him, yes, but it is not enough to merely read them. Behind these words stand a mighty Savior who pleads, "Come to me, that I may give you life."

CHRIST IN YOU, YOU IN CHRIST

How can Jesus claim preeminence in all things? The Scriptures declare that "in him all things hold together. And he is the head of the body, the church. He is the beginning, the firstborn from the dead, that in *everything* he might be preeminent" (Colossians 1:17-18). It is this: We are the body of Jesus Christ. Not only are we in Jesus, but His life indwells each Christian. It is these two categories of truth—Christ in you, and you in Christ—that must be understood in order to properly grow in Jesus. For example, when the apostle Paul writes that God has "blessed us *in Christ* with every spiritual blessing" (Ephesians 1:3), it must be understood what it means to be "in Christ" in order to appropriate one's position in Jesus.

Likewise, we must know what it means to have Christ in *us*. Paul writes again of a powerful mystery, which is "Christ in you, the hope of glory" (Colossians 1:27). Jesus stood in the upper room and promised to His disciples that He would make His home within them: "'I will not leave you as orphans; I will come to you. Yet a little while and the world will see me no more, but you will see me. Because I live, you also will live. In that day you will know that I am in my Father, and you in me, and I in you'" (John 14:18-20). Likewise, Jesus has promised—by the agency of the Holy Spirit—to radically transform our lives from the inside out. We desperately need for the Spirit to open our eyes to see what it means to have the person of Christ living His life within us.

It is these two essential ideas—Christ in us, we in Christ—that true spirituality is built upon and will be the content of this book. The Christian life *is* Christ.

21

Divorcing Christianity from the life of Jesus will reduce it to rules and hypocrisy. There is no life apart from the person of Jesus.

In this age of quick fixes and cheap remedies, it is vital that the church understands Christian spirituality. An authentic Christian life only comes by the resurrected life of Jesus Christ working within each one of us. We cannot settle for a Christ-less Christianity. I encourage you to discover, or perhaps rediscover, what Jesus Christ has done on your behalf. It is time to rediscover Jesus. True spirituality awaits.

CHAPTER 02 - RIGHTEOUS IN CHRIST

For our sake he made him to be sin who knew
no sin, so that in him we might become the
righteousness of God. (2 Corinthians 5:21)

THE FALL IN EDEN

"Then the Lord God formed the man of dust from the ground and breathed into his nostrils the breath of life, and the man became a living creature. And the Lord God planted a garden in Eden, in the east, and there he put the man who he had formed" (Genesis 2:7-8). The brief time that Adam and Eve spent in the Garden of Eden was a unique moment in history. The first humans were—at least in the beginning—perfect, and they enjoyed an unhindered fellowship with their Creator. One can only imagine what this time was like for them, to be so close to the Almighty. They could walk with Him in the cool of the day. They could approach God and talk to Him at any moment. But all of that drastically changed when the first humans disobeyed and rebelled against God. There are three tragic results from this story in Genesis that have plagued mankind throughout history, and have only been dealt with through the finished work of Jesus Christ.

The first result caused by the fall was that humanity now had a real moral guilt before God. Before this moment there was nothing affecting the relationship God had with His people, and yet now there was guilt and looming divine judgment. Human disobedience rightly brought sin and condemnation. After God had formed the first humans from dust He told them that they could freely enjoy the fruit from any tree in the garden—except one:

> And the Lord God commanded the man, saying, "You may surely eat of every tree of the garden, but of the tree of the knowledge of good and evil you shall not eat, for in the day that you eat of it you shall surely die." (Genesis 2:16-17)

Eventually Adam and Eve were both deceived by Satan and disobeyed God, eating from the forbidden tree. In doing this they sinned and broke God's law—the very law of the universe. And while no person today has eaten from the tree of the knowledge of good and evil, the problem of sin has persisted. It is a problem that has infected humanity throughout the ages. The apostle Paul writes, "All have sinned and fall short of the glory of God" (Romans 3:23). Later, we read that sin brings only condemnation and death. "For the wages of sin is death, but the free gift of God is eternal life in Christ Jesus our

Lord" (Romans 6:23). How can Scripture say this? God exists and He is holy. God's law is *based* upon His holy nature. The Lord created a moral universe in which divine justice follows sin. When we sin we break His law, violate His character, and we too are guilty of the penalty of death. This is very serious indeed. Every person has broken God's law and consequently has a true and abiding moral guilt before the Lord. God is a perfect and righteous judge who punishes sin. People hate to hear of this because it is such a frightful thing to know that one day every person who dies in their sins will face the wrath of God. Even while their own consciences scream within them, they put this terrifying thought out of their minds and choose to get on with their lives. But the Bible is clear on this: Every individual is a guilty sinner and needs to atone for their own sins, but lack the power or ability to do so.

There is a second consequence coming out of Eden; one that stems as a result of our sins. It is something everyone experiences. It is the feeling of *shame* brought by our guilt. When the Lord first made Adam and his wife, they had no shame. "And the man and his wife were both naked and were not ashamed" (Genesis 2:25). It is surprising to learn that the first humans moved about paradise not caring that they were naked. In fact, they did not even *know* what "naked" meant. They were just as God had created them—without flaw or guilty imperfection. The absence of sin meant there was *no* cause for guilt or shame. Human disobedience changed that. Immediately after they stretched out their fingertips and ate the forbidden fruit, we read that "then the eyes of both were opened, and they knew that they were naked"

(Genesis 3:7). This detail in Genesis reveals much about the state of the human race. Before the fall, humans were the only beings in creation that displayed the image of God. "So God created man in his own image, in the image of God he created him; male and female he created them" (Genesis 1:27). They were in His image, and while they were yet naked, they were not ashamed. But when sin entered the image of God was corrupted. Sin had perverted it. Now there was something within Adam and Eve that was wrong and instinctively knew they needed to cover themselves. After the fall their eyes were opened and they understood the implication of their nakedness, that they had corrupted the image of God which they bore, and they were ashamed.

Sin, guilt, and shame lead to the third consequence of Adam's fall in Eden: A permanent separation from God. After Adam and Eve sinned, after they realized they were now naked and felt the weight of their shame, they heard the sound of God Almighty making His way through the garden. His footsteps must have rang like thunder inside of them; the Holy One approaching His now unholy creatures.

> And they heard the sound of the Lord God walking in the garden in the cool of the day, and the man and his wife hid themselves from the presence of the Lord God among the trees of the garden. (Genesis 3:8)

Our first parents quickly understood that something inside of them had fundamentally changed. Things were not right. We have all experienced this feeling, that there is something inside of us that is broken, something that we're ashamed of. And so we too spend our lives running from Him. Sinful creatures have no place with a holy God.

The separation of man and his wife from their Creator is summed up in one sober moment as God called out to His lost people: "Where are you?" (Genesis 3:9). If we stop and think about this question, we may see how crushing it really is. Why would an all-knowing God not know where to find someone? Of course He knew *where* Adam and Eve were. Instead, God's question in Eden represents a deeper reality, one of infinite melancholy and tragedy. For the first time ever—and for every day after—humanity was now separated from the Lord. No longer was God's dwelling place with man, as before; now sinners would flee from the wrath of a holy God. The final picture we're given is that of two lonely creatures, frightened and huddled together while being driven from paradise, never to return again.

THE BLOOD OF JESUS CHRIST

When speaking of Adam's fall in Eden, we must remember this: These events were in the mind of God for all eternity. Before the foundation of the world the Lord has had a plan on how to redeem sinners from their sins. God's answer to the problem of our sins is the blood of Jesus Christ. The "blood" is the substitutionary death of Jesus on the cross for the remission of our sins. It is the violent and sudden slaughter of the Lamb of God for our forgiveness. John the Baptist spoke of Jesus one day when he saw Christ coming toward him, "Behold, the Lamb of God, who takes away the sins of the world!" (John 1:29). The blood is of utmost importance. It deals with our individual sins and justifies us before a holy God. The blood completely satisfies the wrath of God. This truth of justification by the blood is recorded throughout the Bible:

> God shows his love for us in that while we were still sinners, Christ died for us. Since, therefore, we have now been justified by his blood, much more shall we be saved by him from the wrath of God. (Romans 5:8, 9)

> In him we have redemption through his blood, the forgiveness of our trespasses, according to the riches of his grace. (Ephesians 1:7)

> For in him all the fullness of God was pleased to dwell, and through him to reconcile to himself all things, whether on earth or in heaven, making peace by the blood of his cross. (Colossians 1:19-20)

> Indeed, under the law almost everything is purified with blood, and without the shedding of blood there is no forgiveness of sins (Hebrews 9:22)

God's solution to the fall of humanity—and to all our sins—was Christ's violent death on the cross. And while the fact that Jesus died for our sins is very wonderful indeed, it is vital that we understand the *depth* of what justification means to us, its implications and outworking. We need the Holy Spirit to open the eyes of our hearts to see *why* the blood is such a significant thing. We must move beyond a *superficial* knowledge of doctrine towards a deep understanding that will help us mature spiritually.

THE BLOOD IS FIRST FOR GOD

The shed blood of Jesus Christ is *not* something primarily for us, but for God. The blood is what God accepts as the *one thing* that makes atonement for a man's sins. Consequently, in order to grasp the immense value of the blood, we must know the value that the Lord places on it. Only in the light of God's valuation of the blood can we understand the value that the blood of Jesus has towards us.

There are two illustrations in the Old Testament that will help us understand how the blood is something first for God. Stories in the Old Testament are often New Testament truths illustrated for us; while the New Testament reveals the truths of the Old Testament (Romans 15:4, 1 Corinthians 10:11). Leviticus 16 describes for us the Day of Atonement. On the Day of Atonement a sin offering was done publicly. This took place outside in the court of the tabernacle. The Lord gave the Israelites clear instructions, however, that no one was allowed *inside* of the tabernacle except for the high priest. The high priest would enter into the tabernacle with the sin offering and would go behind the veil into the Holy Place. This is significant because within the Holy Place was the Ark of the Covenant, on top of which sat the mercy seat, where the presence of God was said to dwell. No one was ever allowed to enter into the Holy Place—only the high priest, once a year and only after elaborate ceremonial preparation. This separation was for the safety of Israel and the high priest, for sinners cannot stand before a holy God without being destroyed: "And the Lord spoke to Moses, 'Tell Aaron your brother not to come at any time into the Holy Place inside the veil, before the mercy seat that is on the ark, *so that he may not die*'" (Leviticus 16:2). The high priest entered into the Holy Place for one reason: To present the blood of the sin offering to God in order to make atonement for the sins of the people:

> "Then he shall kill the goat of the sin offering that is for the people and bring its blood inside the veil… sprinkling it over the mercy seat and in front of the mercy seat. Thus he shall make atonement for the Holy Place, because of the uncleannesses of the people of Israel and because of their transgressions, all their sins." (Leviticus 16:15-16)

This was all done in *secret*, behind the veil, away from the very people who the high priest was making atonement for. The blood was not for the congregation to see, but was presented *to the Lord* as a sin offering. The blood was for God.

A second picture is found in the book of Exodus. On the day of the Passover the people were instructed to take a spotless lamb, slaughter it, and paint the blood on the doorposts and the lintels of the house (Exodus 12:7). During the night, the people were safe inside their homes while the Lord Almighty passed over them. God told His people, "The blood shall be a sign for you, on the houses where you are. And when I see the blood, I will pass over you" (Exodus 12:13). No one inside of the house could see the blood. Only God could see it. And while the blood was a sign to the Israelites, the blood was something that God needed first to see Himself in order that He would pass over that household. Paul later explains Christ as *our* Passover lamb (1 Corinthians 5:7). In the same manner that God passed over the Israelites in Egypt when He saw the blood of the land, so when He sees the blood of the Lamb of God His judgment passes over us.

So there is a common thread running through both of these illustrations, and even into the New Testament with the blood of Jesus Christ: It is that while we are certainly aware of the blood and its workings, and it has atoned for our sins; the blood is something that was first presented to God, to satisfy *His* divine justice.

THE BLOOD PAYS THE PRICE

The shed blood of Christ is first for God. He forgives our sins, not because He overlooks them, not because He ignores them, but because He *sees* the blood of Jesus Christ and is satisfied. A holy, all-knowing God cannot simply forget sins. Every sin ever committed will be paid for in the end—either by the mighty blood of Jesus or by the second death in the lake of fire (Revelation

20:14-15). The Lord is a righteous judge and will not allow sin to endure. The first mention of blood in the Bible is about the shedding of *innocent* blood, of when Cain murdered his brother, Abel.

> And the Lord said, "What have you done? The voice of your brother's blood is crying to me from the ground." (Genesis 4:10)

In contrast, the last mention of blood is concerned with avenging the wicked by shedding their *own* blood:

> He [Jesus] is clothed in a robe dipped in blood, and the name by which he is called is The Word of God. (Revelation 19:13)

The first blood shed is that of an innocent man; the last shed blood is when a holy God is avenging wicked men. The souls of the martyrs call out to the Father from under the altar in heaven, "O Sovereign Lord, holy and true, how long before you will judge and avenge our blood on those who dwell on the earth?" (Revelation 6:10). In the end all accounts will be balanced, each person according to his deeds. That is why it is essential that God sees the blood. He sees the shed blood of Jesus and His holy wrath is satisfied.

It is God's divine justice that demands a sinless life be forfeited for sins. God is the one to whom the blood is presented as proof that a life violently was ended for the remission of sins. And when God sees the blood, He is satisfied. Jesus Christ was the *only* sinless sacrifice for our sins. The Lamb of the world, such seamless beauty, was one of limitless perfection. He was "like that of a lamb without blemish or spot" (1 Peter 1:19). The good news of the gospel is that God has accepted the blood, as "a fragrant offering and sacrifice" (Ephesians 5:2). On the cross Jesus took our place and endured the divine judgment that we deserved. God's full wrath was poured out upon the Savior in order to atone for the sins of the world. And if any person would repent and put their faith in Jesus Christ, His blood will cover their sins as well, and the kingdom of heaven is open to them. They will escape the second death. They will walk in the holy city, where God will dwell with them (Revelation 21:2-3).

Having thus been redeemed by the blood of Jesus, as we grow in the Lord we must appropriate this truth by resting in the finished work of Christ, because it will bring peace to our hearts. God's wrath has been poured out upon the Son and His divine justice has been satisfied. What does this mean for us? It means that now there is zero condemnation towards us who believe: "There is therefore now no condemnation for those who are in Christ Jesus" (Romans 8:1). The blood has washed away all of our unrighteousness.

This truth has a very practical outworking. There are many believers who, even after coming to the Lord, still feel guilty and defeated. I was certainly once a person like that. As a young Christian, any spiritual vigor and strength that I possessed was strangled out of me by guilt. I would have done *anything* to get myself out from underneath the guilt that was crushing me. The problem was—at least for me—that I was trying to *sense* the truth of my own righteous standing before God. I was trying to gauge my righteousness before God on myself and my own perceived goodness. I was reaching my hands out in dimly lit room, trying to *feel* that God had now accepted me. Many Christians do this. They are trying to feel *subjectively* the value of the blood. But it does not work that way. We must trust that the blood has cleansed us from all unrighteousness because God has told us it is so. It is only when we rest upon truth—upon objective reality—that our feelings will be transformed and aligned with what the Bible teaches.

SHAME

The author of Hebrews writes something interesting about Jesus and His crucifixion. He explains that Jesus, "for the joy that was set before him endured the cross, *despising the shame*" (Hebrews 12:2). The cross was a shameful death. The condemned person was stripped naked, beaten, and then stretched across two boards and nailed to them. The crucified were mocked and spat upon while they were forced to suffer and die in slow agony. Crucifixion was such a horrific form of execution that it was forbidden for Roman citizens to be crucified. And to the Jew, they believed that "everyone who is hanged on a tree" is cursed by God (Galatians 3:13). We cannot fully grasp how shameful of a death crucifixion was. And yet Jesus, by His own authority, *allowed* Himself to be killed this way. This is something altogether amazing; that the eternal Word of God would become flesh, and would allow Himself to be subject to torment, agony, and even shame.

We all have experienced the bitter pangs of shame. We all know what it's like to commit evil in the darkness, only to later feel its shameful consequences. Yet in contrast to this, there is some very good news: Jesus took all of our sins and bore them on the cross. He took all the wicked deeds we have ever committed and are ashamed of, and paid for them by His blood. The Savior spoke from the cross, "'It is finished,'" (John 19:30), cancelling not only our condemnation but also our shame.

Our redemption was not purchased cheaply. Whenever we speak of redemption, it is always in connection with the payment of a price for the purchase of a slave or prisoner. *And there is always a cost to the redeemer in the act of redemption.* Even in the Old Testament, when the Lord redeemed His people from Egypt, there is an emphasis on the cost to the Redeemer: "Say therefore to the people of Israel, 'I am the Lord, and I will bring you out from under the burdens of the Egyptians, and I will deliver you from slavery to them, and I will redeem you with an outstretched arm and with great acts of judgment'" (Exodus 6:6). And our Kinsman-Redeemer, Jesus Christ, paid a great price for our redemption. He did so not only physically, but in bearing our guilt and shame.

In Hebrews it is written that the redeemed have "hearts sprinkled clean from an evil conscience" (Hebrews 10:22). It is a marvelous thing that the blood also works in a way as to cleanse our consciences, or else we might go about guiltless, yet always feeling guilty; pure, yet feeling profane; spotless, yet with dirty consciences. And while there was a time when our consciences *did* torment us; that our sins remained with the wrath of a vengeful God ready to befall us, that day is now gone. The blood of Jesus—in cleansing us from unrighteousness—has abolished condemnation once for all, along with any sense of guilt and shame we had stemming from our evil consciences.

RIGHTEOUS IN CHRIST

We have discussed how the Lord has taken all of our iniquities—all our sins and dirty deeds that we are ashamed of—and placed them on Jesus. Christ was punished for our sins on the cross. His blood paid the price of our sins and purchased our redemption. But even more than that, God has provided for us a perfect righteousness in His Son. He has made us *right*; He has made us *acceptable*. Hear the words of Paul the apostle:

> For our sake he [God] made him [Jesus] to be sin who knew no sin, so that in him we might become the righteousness of God. (2 Corinthians 5:21)

Jesus Christ not *only* paid for our sins in His death; He gave us a perfect righteousness, His own righteousness. We see this very plainly at the beginning of His earthly ministry, when Jesus visited John the Baptist in order to be baptized by him.

> Then Jesus came from Galilee to the Jordan to John, to be baptized by him. John would have prevented him, saying "I need to be baptized by you, and do you come to me?" But Jesus answered him,

> "Let it be so now, for thus it is fitting for us to *fulfill all righteousness*." (Matthew 3:13-15)

In this act we see that Christ needed to fulfill all righteousness. In His perfect obedience, Jesus fulfilled every demand made by the Law of God and thus had a righteousness-fulfilling life. More than that, He *identified* Himself with us and gave us His own righteousness. This He did for our sake. Consequently, Christ became our substitute in *two* senses. First, He took our rightful place of judgment, having had the wrath of God poured out upon Him on the cross. We deserved that. We deserved to die for our sins and be eternally separated from God. But even while we were God's enemies, He loved us very much and Jesus chose to die for us. He became our curse (Galatians 3:13) and our condemnation (Romans 8:3). That is the first way that Christ is our substitute. The second sense in which Christ is our substitution is that Jesus, in His life of obedience, *became* our perfection. He *is* our righteousness.

> He is the source of your life in Christ Jesus, whom God made our wisdom and our *righteousness* and sanctification and redemption. (1 Corinthians 1:30)

Christ's righteousness was imputed to us. Imputation is when God counts sinners to be righteous through faith in Jesus. It is entirely on the basis of Christ's perfect blood and righteousness, plus nothing on our part. This righteousness is a very precious gift. It is God's great gift to us (Romans 4:4-5), by His grace, to be accepted by faith alone.

Imputation is a term connected with crediting. Our transgressions have been credited to Christ; likewise we've been credited with Jesus' righteousness. And while the concept of imputation *includes* crediting, it is an even deeper thing than just that. Jesus Christ became so radically associated with our sins that the Bible goes as far as to say that Christ was "*made* sin" (2 Corinthians 5:21). And likewise we have been so radically identified with Jesus Christ and His righteousness that we have become the very righteousness of God *in* Christ. We are not merely considered right with God, we are *actually* right with God! This truth of righteousness, if allowed to speak to our hearts, will provide us with much peace—peace as wide as the seas, or peace like shoes for our naked feet.

A parenthetical note needs to be added here in order to avoid error. When Christ was made sin on our behalf, it was *not* in the sense that He morally became a sinner. Jesus did not become an immoral person in His death. Likewise, in becoming God's righteousness, we don't become morally righteous or perfect. Christ's righteousness does not become the moral quality of our souls. This is evident not only from Scripture (1 John 1:8), but also from our own experience as well. While we are righteous in Jesus as a matter of position, we still have many habits, attitudes, and behaviors that are sinful and the Lord will work out in our lives as He conforms us to the image of His Son.

In the person of Jesus Christ we have become the very righteousness of God. This is a fantastic truth, and I will tell you why: While many Christians know that God loves them, they mistakenly feel that He still doesn't quite *accept* them. They feel that their heavenly Father is disappointed in them, or they cannot approach Him because they're not doing enough good works. Instead of drawing near to the throne of grace with confidence in times of need (Hebrews 4:16), the Father to them is distant and dismayed, just waiting for them to get their act together. This is the way many Christians think about their relationship with God. Their faith is a sad roller coaster ride. Many people in the church today have accepted Christ as their Savior, only to turn around in a gray swirl and toil endlessly to get God to accept them in return.

This, however, is far from the reality that we have in Christ. Because of what the Son has done—because of His blood and righteousness—we are now as *righteous and as acceptable to God as the Lord Jesus Christ Himself.* This is a reality for all Christians—right now. Even at this very moment, while you read these words and hold these frail pages in your hands, you are righteous. You are acceptable. Not because of anything you've done, or could ever hope to do, but because you are righteous *in* Christ. My prayer is that the Holy Spirit will open the eyes of your heart, that this truth penetrates you and that you feel it in the very fiber or your marrow, even through your calloused bones. This truth of righteousness will guard your heart greatly, like a breastplate or a suite of armor. It will keep you from fainting under the heavy sense of your own weaknesses and imperfections. Hold this truth tightly to your chest.

We are now acceptable to God. Even more than that, because we are "in" the Son, and He is a source of endless delight to the Father, we are now a source of delight to God as well. The Father has "blessed us in the Beloved" (Ephesians 1:6). Yet to get a more complete grasp on the subject, we need to understand what it means to be "in Christ." It is a term used throughout the New Testament. The Holy Spirit must illuminate this truth to us, if we are to understand what it means to have "become the righteousness of God… in Him" (2 Corinthians 5:21). It is only by virtue of being in Jesus that we've been made righteousness. I will elaborate on this subject further in a later chapter, but for now a good working understanding is that to be "in Christ" is to be radically identified with Jesus in His life, death, and resurrection.

An excellent picture of this truth is an analogy of a letter sent in an envelope. If you were to write a note to a dear friend, then seal the letter in an envelope, the letter would then be "in" the envelope. While the letter is inside the envelope, it has no identity apart from the envelope. Everywhere the envelope goes, the letter must go as well. Likewise, everything that happens to the envelope happens to the letter. If you were to mail them to the city, they must both go there together. Whatever experience the envelope goes through, the letter must go through as well. In the very same way, our lives have been so entwined with the person of Jesus Christ that we are now essentially regarded as one. Our identity *is* Christ. Jesus is our all in all. His life is our life. We must never think of ourselves apart from Him. This is what it means to be in Christ.

A person may ask, "How do I get to be in Christ? What must I do to get 'into' Him?" And the truth is we couldn't work ourselves into Christ, even if we wanted to. Not on our own efforts, at least. But the wonderful news is that we don't need to get into Christ. No, God has already done it for us! The apostle Paul wrote to the church in Corinth:

> But *by His doing* you are in Christ Jesus,
> who became to us wisdom from God,
> and righteousness, and sanctification, and
> redemption. (1 Corinthians 1:30 NASB)

It was by God's own doing that we are in Christ. Yes, there is a bit of a mystery in this. Yet one way or another, God has placed us into His Son. In doing this, Christ has not only become our righteousness, but Jesus is now our wisdom, He is our sanctification, and He is our redemption. Jesus has become to us all things.

One last illustration about righteousness must be explained. Immediately before casting Adam and Eve out of Eden, God did something strange yet wonderful: "And the Lord God made for Adam and his wife garments of skins and clothed them" (Genesis 3:21). What the Lord did was He slaughtered a little animal, and from its skins He made Adam and Eve some clothes. God *clothed* their nakedness, and I love Him for it, because it is a picture of the Savior. God has done the same thing for us in Christ, for whoever has put their faith in Jesus has *put on* Christ. "For as many of you were baptized into Christ have put on Christ" (Galatians 3:23). We are no longer naked, with our shamefulness exposed, but we are now *clothed* with Jesus. It is yet another picture of how Christ has become our identity now; having become our righteousness and wisdom and sanctification and so on. We must never forget: When God sees us—for only He has eyes to see us

41

as we *really* are—we are righteous; as righteous and acceptable to Him as Jesus Christ.

ENTERING THE HOLY OF HOLIES

One of the most troubling obstacles that resulted from the fall of the human race was that it created a violent separation from God. And while there are a number of passages in Scripture illustrating how the blood of Jesus has redeemed people for God, I'd like explore the idea of reconciliation through the typology of the ancient tabernacle of Israel. The tabernacle wasn't the *true* tent of God, but only a physical representation of a deeper spiritual reality. The author of Hebrews writes:

> They [the high priests] serve a copy and
> shadow of the heavenly things. For when
> Moses was about to erect the tent, he was
> instructed by God, saying, "See that you
> make everything according to the pattern
> that was shown you on the mountain."
> (Hebrews 8:5)

When Moses spent forty days alone with the Almighty on Mt. Sinai, God gave him a glimpse of the *real* tabernacle (the one in heaven) and told him to be careful when he built the shadow (the tabernacle on earth), that it was an accurate copy of the heavenly tabernacle. Notice the layout of the tabernacle and what each room represented:

For a tent was prepared, the first section,

> in which were the lampstand and the table and the bread of the Presence. It is called the Holy Place. Behind the second curtain was a second section called the Most Holy Place, having the golden altar of incense and the Ark of the Covenant... Above it were the cherubim of glory overshadowing the mercy seat. Of these things we cannot now speak in detail. (Hebrews. 9:2-5)

The first section was the Holy Place, and further inside of the tabernacle—separated by a huge curtain—was the Most Holy Place, which is sometimes called the Holy of Holies. The priests could enter regularly into the Holy Place to perform their ritual duties, but they could *never* enter into the Most Holy Place! Only the high priest could go behind the curtain into the Holy of Holies, and but once a year after elaborate ceremonial cleansing and preparation (Hebrews 9:7). By this setup the Spirit was showing us that the holy places were not yet opened (Hebrews 9:8). This is very tragic indeed, because inside the Holy of Holies was the mercy seat—which represented the very presence of the Lord, where God Himself was seated in glorious splendor (Exodus 25:22). *The sins of the people kept them from entering into God's holy presence.*

But what happened the *very* moment Christ was crucified?

> And Jesus cried out again with a loud voice and yielded up his spirit. And behold, *the curtain of the temple was torn in*

two, from top to bottom. And the earth
shook, and the rocks were split. (Matthew
27:50-51)

This is what happened: Jesus' body was broken like the
bread we remember Him with. And through that opened
curtain of His flesh, the very curtain of the temple was
torn in half. The Holy of Holies was now *opened* by the
blood of Jesus. This is fantastic news; at the *exact* moment
our Lord was crucified the veil blocking the Most Holy
Place was torn right down the middle! The blood of Christ
had accomplished exactly what it had promised to do.
Jesus did away with the sins of His people and gave them
access to the Holy of Holies—the very presence of God.

What is more striking about the accomplishment of
the blood was the speed of it. The atonement worked
immediately and without fail. Within the same breath of
our Lord's death the temple curtain was done away with.
Thus at that very moment in history *anyone* who had faith
in Christ, from least to greatest, could then enter the holy
places—by the blood—and be in the presence of God.
The same is true of us! Right now as you read this very
sentence you have full access to the Lord by the blood of
Christ. *Right now*—at this very moment! As a believer in
Christ you can enter into God's presence with confidence
and a clear conscience. You can experience the fullness of
joy that only His presence can bring; you can find help in
times of need, and experience the hope and peace He so
lovingly bestows on His children. "Let us then with
confidence draw near to the throne of grace, that we may
receive mercy and find grace to help in time of need"
(Hebrews 4:16).

This is what Paul meant when he wrote to the Ephesians, telling them that we who were once far off have been "brought near by the blood of Christ" (Ephesians 2:13). Let me ask you only this: Are you living in the "nearness" that the blood has purchased for you? That is what the writer of Hebrews urges us to do. All the work has been finished. By the blood of Jesus we can now draw near to God and walk with Him daily. The hostility and separation from God has been dealt with, once for all time, in the perfect sacrifice of Jesus, and the mistakes of our first parents have been undone.

Consequently, the matter of access and nearness to God has two phases: An initial one and a more progressive one. Initially, we are justified by the blood and are brought near to the Lord. This is a matter of our standing before Him. In this phase the Lord has redeemed His children and established a relationship with them. But there is another phase which is really a practical outworking of our newly purchased nearness:

> Therefore, brothers, since we have confidence to enter the holy places by the blood of Jesus, by the new and living way that he opened for us through the curtain, that is, through his flesh... let us draw near with a true heart in full assurance of faith, with our hearts sprinkled clean from an evil conscience. (Hebrews 10:19-20, 22)

So while we have been first brought near to God by the blood of the Lamb, the writer of Hebrews encourages us to keep drawing near to God. We have been reconciled to Him, now we must seek and pursue our Redeemer. That is now our joy and heartbeat. Yet, what we must realize is that in both phases, our approach to God is always on the same basis. *It is always by the blood of Jesus.* We must never attempt to enter God's presence by any other means. We shouldn't feel that we can approach God one day because we have been extra good. Likewise, we shouldn't feel that we can't approach God on another day because we have been bad. No, we always enter into the holy places by the blood of Jesus. I hope you are beginning to see just how valuable the blood really is!

The apostle Peter speaks about it in this manner: "You were ransomed from the futile ways inherited from your forefathers, not with perishable things such as silver or gold, but with the precious blood of Christ" (1 Peter 1:18-19). Let me ask you this: How much wealth would you need before you could *buy* your way into the presence of the holy God? Would all the wealth and jewels of kings be enough? How many tons of gold or silver would it take to pay for your sins? Of course these questions are absurd, because there is no amount of wealth, nor is there anything we could ever do that could restore our relationship with God. The Scriptures say, "Indeed, under the law almost everything is purified with blood, and without the shedding of blood there is no forgiveness of sins" (Hebrews 9:22). It is *only* the blood of Jesus Christ that can wash away our sins and bring us near to God. Likewise, it is only on the basis of the perfect blood of Jesus that we ever approach God. And this blood never changes, never wears out, and never fails.

WHEN WE SIN

The question inevitably arises: What happens when we sin? We are the righteousness of God in Christ, and then sin re-enters, is all now lost? Thankfully the Bible is a practical and honest book. It does not shy away from things, not even this. The apostle John writes in his first letter concerning this:

> This is the message we have heard from him and proclaim to you, that God is light, and in him is no darkness at all. If we say we have fellowship with him while we walk in darkness, we lie and do not practice the truth. But if we walk in the light, as he is in the light, we have fellowship with one another, and the blood of Jesus cleanses us from all sin. If we say we have no sin, we deceive ourselves, and the truth is not in us. If we confess our sins, he is faithful and just to forgive us our sins and to cleanse us from all unrighteousness. (1 John 1:5-9)

Before we go into an in-depth discussion on the way of restoration and cleansing, a few important distinctions must be made. Many people read this passage and automatically equate walking in darkness with having fallen into sin, but this is not quite true. A Christian sins *because* they are walking in darkness. A person can be a believer in Christ and still have times and even seasons of their lives when they walk in dark places. This is what John is telling us. If that person claims to have fellowship with God, and is still walking in darkness, then that person is a liar. "If we say we have fellowship with him while we walk in darkness, we lie and do not practice the truth" (1 John 1:6). Darkness is simply the absence of light—in this case the very light of God. A Christian who is walking in darkness has turned away from fellowship with Him. He has shut God out of his experience, like a man would turn off a light switch. When this happens their life is instantly flooded with darkness and they are not having fellowship with the One who describes Himself as only the purest light. And this darkness *leads* to sinning.

Another distinction must be made: There is a crucial difference between having a *relationship* with God and having *fellowship* with Him. A relationship is when a person has responded by faith to the gospel by repenting of their sins and receiving Christ, and thus has been adopted into the family of God. "But all who did receive him, who believed in his name, he gave the right to become children of God" (John 1:12). Every Christian has a relationship with the Lord. Fellowship, however, is when a person is *experiencing* the life of God by the presence of the Holy Spirit. In relationship everything that is of Christ is *potentially* yours; in fellowship you are *actually* drawing upon the life of Jesus in your current experience. With those two distinctions being made, let us move on.

The way of cleansing after a Christian has sinned is nothing new. It is still by the blood of Jesus Christ. But it is important to note that this is *not* a re-justification. We are not lost when we sin; our justification is once for all time. "For by a single offering he has *perfected for all time* those who are being sanctified" (Hebrews 10:17). Perhaps the greatest truth of justification is that, as Christians, Jesus has made us perfect *forever*. Even when we sin, God still holds us; we do not have a lost relationship. But when we sin our fellowship with God has been affected. After sinning, we must confess our sins or else continue walking in darkness as long as we harbor sin in our heart.

The answer that John gives us is very straight forward: It is to confess our sins and return to walking in the light.

> If we confess our sins, he is faithful and just to forgive us our sins and to cleanse us from all unrighteousness. (1 John 1:9)

As we are walking in the light, the blood of Jesus is continuously cleansing us from all sin. This is a present-tense cleansing, done instantaneously, all the time. Again, this is not a re-justification! The idea here is that the world can be a defiling place. We defile ourselves, and need a continuous cleansing to remain holy in the inner temple of the human heart. A good picture of this sort of cleansing is given to us in John 13, during the last supper. While Jesus was in the upper room with His disciples, He tied a towel around His waist, took a basin of water, and began to wash their feet. As He made His way around to each disciple, Peter became unsettled by what Jesus was doing.

> He came to Simon Peter, who said to him, "Lord, do you wash my feet?" Jesus answered him, "What I am doing you do not understand now, but afterwards you will understand." Peter said to him, "You

shall never wash my feet." (John 13:6-8)

Simon Peter thought it was wrong for his master to wash his feet. He felt that the lesser should serve the greater. And while Jesus did explain that Peter would not understand at that time, He gave Simon Peter a solemn rebuke. "Jesus answered him, 'If I do not wash you, you have no share with me.' Simon Peter said to him, Lord, not my feet only but also my hands and my head!'" (John 13:8-9). Here is the truth of cleansing. If Christ doesn't wash us—if His blood doesn't justify us from all our sins—then we can having *nothing* to do with Him. After hearing Jesus make this statement, Peter urged Him to not only wash his feet, but to also cleanse his hands and his head. He wanted to be washed all over. He wanted Jesus. Yet Christ corrected Peter, "Jesus said to him, 'The one who has bathed does not need to wash, except for his feet, *but is completely clean*'" (John 13:10). That picture is *exactly* what a Christian's cleansing is like. The first washing that Jesus has given us is our justification, making us perfect forever. We are "completely clean." But there is a practical outworking of this truth. Jesus has told us that the person who has bathed does not need another bath, only his feet need washing. So we see that as we walk through this world the blood gives us a continuous cleansing—a repeated washing of our feet.

What is required when we sin is simply to *confess*, and that God will be faithful, He will cleanse us from all unrighteousness. It is important to see just what confession is: Confessing our sins is not the same thing as asking for forgiveness—we've already been forgiven! What confession means is for us to agree with God that our specific sin is *sin*, and to turn away from it. That is all that is required. Guilt feelings won't restore fellowship with the Lord, neither will acts of penance. Nothing else is required beyond confessing our sin and turning away from it.

In my life I have learned that confession is best done immediately, as soon as I realize that I have done wrong. The same is true for everyone. *There is no reason to wait.* It is absurd to walk in darkness, harbor a specific sin in your heart, and have it lead you deeper down a broken path, deeper into sin. In fact, if we wait to confess, we will only make things worse and allow ourselves to be led into bondage. No, do not hesitate; confess your sins and look back to the perfect face of Jesus Christ.

Another point of emphasis should be added. We ought to be very deliberate in confessing *specific* sins. It is not enough to say in general terms that we have sinned; no, we must be open and willing to call our specific sins *sin*. There is a tendency—at least in my own journey—to confess to God only vaguely, all the while holding on to a specific sin. We must be very honest with ourselves before the Lord, so that when the Spirit is prompting us we are willing to confess our specific sins and to return to walking in the light.

I would like to say here that I am very thankful for Jesus' parable of the Prodigal Son in Luke 15. Here was a boy who was *deep* in sin, even by the world's standards. He demanded his portion of the family inheritance and in doing so told his father that he wanted nothing to do with him, that he wished his father was dead. He left and squandered all of his wealth until his life was left in the deepest ocean of despair. He ended up in the mire, eating the slop that was only fed to swine. And what happened when the son finally came to his senses and wanted to return home? His father was waiting for him. We may never fully understand this, but the father was desperately longing for the son to return home. He was ready to throw his arms around his boy and celebrate his return. The lesson we must learn from this story is this: There isn't any sin too great that the blood of Christ can't cleanse us and restore our fellowship with *our* Heavenly Father. God loves us very much, more than we could ever grasp. He is a great God. And if we would but confess and turn from our sins and look back to Him, He will always welcome us back.

CHAPTER 03 – CRUCIFIED WITH CHRIST

I have been crucified with Christ. It is no longer
I who live, but Christ who lives in me.
(Galatians 2:20)

OUR NATURE IN ADAM

We have discussed the remarkable truth of our justification, how we are now completely righteous in Christ. By the blood of Jesus guilt and wrath have been turned away; righteousness and peace now reign in our hearts. Having an assurance of righteousness in Him and justification by His blood will provide a firm foundation and a starting point to explore true Christian spirituality. And while justification is the essential starting point, for without it there is no peace with God, it is just that—a starting point. Just as the day of a man's birth is in one sense the most important day of his life—for without it nothing else could follow—a man cannot dwell forever on the meaning of his birth. After that he must get along with his life. Likewise, as Christians we have had a second birth (John 3:3-7). And while justification is the *most* important truth of our union with Jesus Christ, there is even more to Christianity than only justification. Christians are called to "work out your own salvation with fear and trembling" (Philippians 2:12). Christ is our righteousness, yes, and He is our sanctification as well (1 Corinthians 1:30).

Quite often, when a Christian is very young in their faith, there is a tendency for them to become troubled by the things they *do*. After their conversion, their consciences may be awaked to the many sinful habits they have harbored during their lifetime. There are attitudes they just can't change. No matter how they try, they can't stop making choices that leave themselves feeling broken and ashamed. They struggle and still hurt others and themselves. They only know the "sin that clings so closely" (Hebrews 12:1) and nothing of the grace and truth that comes through Jesus Christ. These never-ending struggles can strangle away any peace that has sprouted in their lives. While in one moment the young Christian rejoices that their sins are forgiven, yet at the same time their struggle is more real, their defeats more crushing, and their consciences are heightened as they work endlessly to get their lives in order. Some delude themselves into thinking that if only they could overcome a few apparent flaws, then all would be well. Others simply give up.

I remember many tiresome nights as a young Christian in my late teens, even into my early twenties, where I would lay on my bed, staring at the lonely ceiling, praying that I would eventually fall asleep. I would be tormented by my conscience, overcome by all the sins I committed that day, even though I knew I shouldn't have done any of them. Also I would think up a long list of things I believed a Christian ought to be doing, and how I had done almost *none* of those things, and how my Christianity was probably a sham and it was only a matter of time before everyone found out. So what I would do is this: Every evening I would plead with God, vowing that tomorrow I would double my efforts and do everything right. I would dust off my Bible and starting reading it, and I would pray, and do all the other things that I thought any sanctimonious saint ought to be doing. Also, I would give up all the crumby habits that left me feeling so ashamed. I genuinely felt that if I could string together enough of these days, then I would finally be the real thing, the sort of Christian that even Jesus might be proud of. How foolish I was in my youth! I quickly found out a terrible fact: No matter how much I wanted to do right or how hard I tried, I just couldn't do it. I was a failure. All the good just wouldn't come out of me; and the evil that I did not want to do was what I kept on doing. And so I began to despair of myself. My heart echoed the apostle Paul:

> So I find it to be a law that when I want to do right, evil lies close at hand. For I delight in the law of God, in my inner being, but I see in my members another law waging war against the law of my mind and making me captive to the law of sin that dwells in my members. Wretched man that I am! Who will deliver me from this body of death? (Romans 7:21-24)

I do not believe that my experience was unique. I am convinced that there are countless Christians, both young and old, whose lives are not much different than mine was. These are people right now who lead lives of quiet desperation. And yet one thing the Bible has shown me is this: It is not what we *do* that is the problem. The problem actually comes from what we *are*. The fundamental problem with man is man himself. This is what Scripture teaches. Humans are by nature sinners. The apostle Paul writes in the book of Romans that this is because of our connection with the first man, Adam, when he sinned in Eden:

> Therefore, just as sin came into the world
> through one man, and death through sin,
> and so death spread to all men because all
> sinned... As the trespass of one led to the
> condemnation of all men... For as by one
> man's disobedience the many were made
> sinners. (Romans 5:12, 18, 19)

Because Adam sinned in the garden, all men were made sinners. Every person now has a nature that *compels* them to sin.

If a person were to make a careful study of the creation account in Genesis, they would find an interesting pattern: After almost every day of creation, God pauses and after looking over all that He had made that day, He declares that "it was good." God separated the light from the darkness, and it was good. He created the earth and the seas, and it was good. He created the plants and the trees, and that was good too. And so on, everything was good, it was all good. But on the sixth day of creation—the day the Lord created man—we are told something different: "So God created man in his own image, in the image of God he created him, male and female He created them" (Genesis 1:27). And we're told that on the end of *that* day, "God saw everything that he had made, and behold, it was very good" (Genesis 1:31). Not just good, but *very* good. Here is a hint that mankind was fundamentally different than the rest of the created order—human beings were made in the image of God. And the fact that man was made after God's own image was *very* good.

Scripture is careful to reflect on the idea that man was created in the image of God again, just before discussing the descendants of Adam. Remember, this passage comes immediately after the fall in Eden. And this time we are confronted with a striking difference:

> When God created man, he made him in the likeness of God... When Adam had lived 130 years, he fathered a son *in his own likeness, after his image*, and named him Seth. (Genesis 5:1, 3)

The mentioning of man being made "in the likeness of God" next to Adam having a son "in his *own* likeness, after his image" was not a mere coincidence. No, the Spirit is showing something here, emphasizing *twice* that Adam had a son after his own likeness. Likewise, not only was Adam's son in his own likeness, but his grandson bore his image as well, and his great-grandson, and so on. Adam was made of dust, and all his offspring bore his own image: "As was the man of dust, so also are those who are of dust" (1 Corinthians 15:48). Due to Adam's rebellion in the garden, a fundamental change took place not only in his own nature, but *all* of humanity as well. This is what Paul was writing about in Romans, stating, "For as by one man's disobedience the many were made sinners" (Romans 5:19). Due to our connection with our first ancestor, Adam, everyone was constituted a sinner by *nature*, unable to please God in any way. The family likeness has been passed down through the generations, all the way to us. Our sinful nature is our inheritance in Adam. In our fallen state, we all are "by nature children of wrath" (Ephesians 2:3). We are all members of a race of people whose own natures compel us to sin.

In light of all this, we must draw an important distinction: We are not sinners because we have committed sins. We sin *because* we are by nature sinners. Every person, without exception, has been constituted a sinner by nature, not by their actions. The behavior of an individual is determined by their identity, not the other way around. It would be of great advantage if we would understand this. Jesus taught, "So, every healthy tree bears good fruit, but the diseased tree bears bad fruit. A healthy tree cannot bear bad fruit, nor can a diseased tree bear good fruit" (Matthew 7:17-18). *The nature of the tree determines the kind of fruit it grows.* It does not matter if we could pick all the fruit off of a diseased tree, or prune it, if it is a diseased tree it will still produce bad fruit. Likewise, if we could hypothetically manage to stop sinning for a span of time, we would still be sinners because we are offspring of Adam. Our fruit would be bad because we are still diseased trees. Adam's disobedience has made all of his descendants into sinners by nature, because all of humanity was connected to Adam when he fell in Eden.

How can the Bible decree that by one man's disobedience all of his descendants are then constituted as sinners? It doesn't seem fair, does it? How can Adam's rebellion in Eden cause such a serious birth defect in the rest of his offspring? Scripture explains this, stating that this is because *we were all in Adam when he fell in the garden.* In the previous chapter we discussed briefly what it means to be "in Christ," that we were placed into Christ by divine action and not as a result of any effort on our part (1 Corinthians 1:30). However, being "in Adam" was *not* a result of God's doing. Instead, every person who has ever been born begins their life being "in Adam." Now we shall explore the idea of being "in Christ" and "in Adam" more in depth to understand the concept more fully.

In God's economy, there are only two people: Adam and Christ. Every person's identity is dictated by one of these two men. The apostle Paul writes of Adam and Jesus in one of his epistles to the church in Corinth:

> The first man was from the earth, a man of dust; the second man is from heaven. As was the man of dust, so also are those who are of the dust, and as is the man of heaven, so also are those who are of heaven. Just as we have borne the image of the man of dust, we shall also bear the image of the man of heaven. (1 Corinthians 15:47-49)

Every person comes into this life bearing the "image of the

man of dust," the fallen nature inherited from Adam. This means that we are born spiritually dead, alienated from the life of God, having natures that compel us to sin. We are slaves to sin. *This is our identity in Adam.* This is the inheritance we have been given from our first father. Adam acted as the federal head of the entire human race. He represented all of humanity when he fell in Eden. So when Adam sinned, he sinned for us all. His fall was also our fall. Consequently, when God declared judgment upon him by withdrawing any capacity Adam had for righteousness, we were all likewise punished. God judged the entire human race in Adam, and all of his descendants were constituted sinners. And there is nothing we can do to escape our condition, for just as each of us was born "in Adam," we shall remain in Adam until the day we die.

THE CROSS OF JESUS CHRIST

As one reads through Romans, they will find that the first eight chapters of the book can naturally be divided into two sections. In the first section, (Romans 1:1–5:11), the apostle is concerned predominantly with the topic of sins. Sins are the individual wrongs that each person has committed against God, when they have broken His commandments and violated His law. Every person daily commits many sins, both in word and deed—these include idolatry, lying, stealing, coveting, sexual immorality, and murder, to name a few. All of these acts are *sins*. It is because of these things that the wrath of God will be poured out upon mankind (Colossians 3:6). The previous chapter showed how the blood of Jesus Christ has paid for all of our sins and has cleansed us from all unrighteousness.

However, in the second division of Romans (Romans 5:12–8:39), Paul shifts his focus. He is no longer concerned so much with sins (plural), but instead gives prominence to the concept of sin (singular). There is a crucial difference between sins and sin. While sins are all the individual acts committed against God, sin is the one principle that causes them. When the apostle Paul discusses *sin*, he is concerned with the power of sin in a person's life. The power of sin is sometimes referred to as "the principle of sin." *It is the power of sin that leads people to commit sins.* Remember, as we have stated before, we commit sins because we are sinners. It is our sinful natures—the power of sin that enslaves a man's will—that drives us to commit sins.

The power of sin is a force that, although it is foreign to us, attempts to take captive the members of our bodies and use them as instruments of unrighteousness. The Scriptures state: "Let not sin therefore reign in your mortal bodies, to make you obey their passions. Do not present your members to sin as instruments of unrighteousness…" (Romans 6:12-13). The power of sin wants to *reign* in our bodies, to make us commit all sorts of wickedness, whether small or grotesque. The principle of sin ultimately derives its power from Satan himself. When Christ was once confronted by the Pharisees at the temple, He rebuked them, declaring, "You are of your father the devil, and your will is to do your father's desires" (John 8:44). While these may sound like harsh words, reserved only for the vilest sinners, the truth is that Jesus could have made this statement about any unbeliever. Every offspring of

Adam is a slave to sin. The Bible teaches that mankind is "following the prince of the power of the air, the spirit that is now at work in the sons of disobedience" (Ephesians 2:2). We are all born as slaves to the power of sin. Humans are in "the snare of the devil, after being captured by him to do his will" (2 Timothy 2:26). And while the blood of Christ washes us all our sins from us, it does *not* remove the power of sin in our lives. No, the blood does not work in that manner. As powerful as the precious blood of Jesus Christ is, it does not change our identity of who we are in Adam, nor does it remove the power of sin from a person's life. Those who are born in Adam as slaves to sin will likewise die in Adam as slaves to sin. Unless a person can change their parentage, there is no hope for deliverance.

Yet the child of God is not without hope. Just as the Lord was not satisfied to leave the children of Israel as slaves in Egypt, but wanted them as Him own possession, our Heavenly Father has not left us as slaves to sin. Romans 6 outlines how God has made provision to deal with the power of sin in our lives. It is a vital passage, and I want to present it in its entirety before exploring each point that the apostle Paul makes here:

> What shall we say then? Are we to continue in sin that grace may abound? Be no means! How can we who died to sin still live in it? Do you not know that all of us who have been baptized into Christ Jesus were baptized into his death? We were buried therefore with him by baptism into death, in order that, just as

Christ was raised from the dead by the glory of the Father, we too might walk in newness of life. For if we have been united with him in a death like His, we shall certainly be united with him in a resurrection like his. We know that our old self was crucified with him in order that the body of sin might be brought to nothing, so that we would no longer be enslaved to sin. For one who has died has been set free from sin. (Romans 6:1-7)

Jesus died, He died, His body was in the tomb, tomb was in the ground, Christ had died for the sins of the world. *And we were united with Jesus in His death.* God's solution to the problem of sin is *not* to remove the power of sin from the life of the Christian (1 John 1:8). Instead, God *kills* the sinner who is enslaved to sin and raises him from the dead in Christ, thus making him a new creation (2 Corinthians 5:17). This new creation is not a slave to sin (Romans 6:7), but now has a moment-by-moment choice to offer his body to God as an instrument of righteousness, or back to sin as an instrument of evil (Romans 6:16). Now, this is not all there is to Christian spirituality, and there is a call to put to death the deeds of the body and to keep in step with the Holy Spirit, among others. But we must first know our position in Jesus Christ before we can understand the implications of death and experience a practical deliverance from sin. Yes, the cold dead body of the Savior of the world was buried in the tomb, and we were buried with Him.

Every Christian—when God placed them into Christ—was also *included* in Jesus' death. We were crucified with Christ. And this is how our heritage in Adam was cut off from us, and how we can begin to find a practical deliverance from the power of sin. By being baptized into the Son, we were also baptized into His *death*: "Do you not know that all of us who have been baptized into Christ Jesus were baptized into his death?" (Romans 6:3). The apostle Paul states it bluntly—"Do you not know?"—showing that this truth is so profound in its implications that every Christian ought to know this truth. We shall work through the details and implications of this passage in the following sections. Yet I want to say here: I think that our crucifixion with Jesus is one of the most precious aspects of being in Christ. It is a truth that has changed my life radically, and continues to change me today. In the cross we see the execution of all things, so when Jesus was lifted up on a hill outside of Jerusalem nearly two-thousand years ago, we were crucified with Him. Paul tells us in a different letter, "that one died for all, therefore *all have died*" (2 Corinthians 5:14).

BAPTISM OF THE HOLY SPIRIT

The word "baptism" is used many times in the passage that is before us now, declaring that we have been baptized into Jesus as well as baptized into His death:

> Do you not know that all of us who have been *baptized* into Christ Jesus were *baptized* into his death? We were buried

> therefore with him by *baptism* into
> death… (Romans 6:3-4)

If we desire to know what it means to be "in Christ," and how the Father has placed us into the Son, we must understand what baptism is to grasp the implications of our baptism into Jesus Christ and into His death, burial, and resurrection.

Historically, the idea of baptism is not found in the Old Testament. It is unique to the New Testament. During the times of Christ the word "baptism" was used in several different ways. For example, it was used to describe a piece of cloth that had been dyed. The cloth was dipped into a vat of thick dye, and when the fabric emerged it was changed into a new color and would have thus been deemed "baptized." From then on the cloth and the dye would always be identified together, as the color of an object is innate to the object itself. The dye and the cloth became as one.

Likewise, the word "baptism" was also used to describe a sunken boat. While at one time the ship was free to sail wherever it desired, after it sank into the ocean it was "baptized" into the sea, never to emerge from its watery grave. The ship was then regarded as part of the ocean, littering the seafloor.

The most common use of the word "baptism" in Jesus' time, however, was in the idea of being *overwhelmed*. For example, when Jesus lamented of His impending death, he referred to it as a baptism. His words here struggle with anguish, as He would eventually cry and plead and sweat blood over the path set before Him:

> "I came to cast fire on the earth, and
> would that it were already kindled! I have
> a baptism to be baptized with, and how
> great is my distress until it is
> accomplished!" (Luke 12:49-50)

We should understand the concept of baptism as a combination of these ideas. Baptism speaks of deep spiritual truth for Christians. It signifies inward cleansing, the remission of sins, new spiritual life, along with the constant presence of the Holy Spirit which was given as a seal forever for those who are in Christ. *Ultimately, it only signifies these things because of the spiritual truth of baptism, that we have been united with Christ in His death, burial and resurrection*: "Do you not know that all of us who have been baptized into Christ Jesus were baptized into his death? We were buried therefore with him by baptism into death..." (Romans 6:3-4). We are as pieces of cloth, being overwhelmed and consumed with a dye which is Christ— from then on we are forever one with Him. We are like scuttled ships, littering the bottom of the sea. No longer can the boats be thought of apart from the water that has overtaken them. Yes, in the same way, Christians have been baptized into Christ, along with His death and resurrection; we now have no identity apart from Jesus.

John the Baptist, whose own reputation was built upon baptism with water, prophesied by saying, "I baptize you with water, but he who is mightier than I is coming, the strap of whose sandals I am not worthy to untie. He will baptize you with the Holy Spirit and with fire" (Luke 3:16). This is the baptism that is before us now in Romans—the baptism of the Holy Spirit—which places us into Christ and brings Christ's resurrection life into us. Paul, in writing to the church in Corinth, explains that Christians have all been baptized into one body, which is the very body of Jesus Christ: "For in one Spirit we were all baptized into one body—Jews or Greeks, slaves or free" (1 Corinthians 12:13).

In Ephesians we are told of seven exclusives in God's reality, seven things of which there is only one each:

> There is one body and one Spirit—just as
> you were called to the one hope that
> belongs to your call—one Lord, one faith,
> one baptism, one God and Father of all,
> who is over all and through all and in all.
> (Ephesians 4:4–6)

From this passage we see that there is only *one* baptism. It is the one baptism we have been discussing, where the Holy Spirit placed us into Christ and united our lives with Jesus. From this we understand that there is a vital difference between the *ceremony* of baptism and the *spiritual reality* that it represents. The ceremony of baptism by water is only a symbol of the one true baptism, the spiritual reality, baptism of the Holy Spirit.

There are a few illustrations of baptism in the Bible which may solidify our thinking as to what it means to have been baptized into Jesus Christ and His death. The Spirit of God must illuminate this precious truth to us, for our unity with Jesus Christ in His death changes *everything*. The first illustration alludes to Moses, when the Israelites crossed the Red Sea with him:

> I want you to know, brothers, that our
> fathers were all under the cloud, and all
> passed through the sea, all were *baptized*
> *into Moses* in the cloud and in the sea. (1
> Corinthians 10:1-2)

In this picture the Israelites, while escaping from Egypt, were identified with Moses as they passed through the Red Sea. In this story from Exodus, the people of Israel were escaping their old lives of slavery in Egypt. As the Israelites made their way through the sea, the Egyptian army was close in pursuit. God had provided a miracle through His servant Moses by parting the sea and allowing His children to pass. When Israel finally made it safely across, the passage closed, and the sea violently consumed the Egyptians so that none of them remained.

A second picture is found in one of the apostle Peter's epistles, speaking of the ark of Noah:

> God's patience waited in the days of
> Noah, while the ark was being prepared,
> in which a few, that is, eight persons,
> were brought safely through water.
> *Baptism, which corresponds to this, now saves*
> *you*, not as a removal of dirt from the
> body but as an appeal to God for a good
> conscience, through the resurrection of
> Jesus Christ. (1 Peter 3:20-21)

In this illustration the family of Noah entered safely into the ark, and then the terrifying flood came and destroyed all the wicked people dwelling on the earth. And the ark is a *type* of Christ. We were baptized into Him. We were crucified with Him, buried with Him, and finally rose with Him. I do not think it's a coincidence that Noah came out of the ark on the same calendar date that Jesus rose from the dead. And just as the Red Sea destroyed the Egyptians, and God wiped all the wicked people from the face of the earth in a great flood, our old identity in Adam was done away with in the death of Jesus—we are now new creatures in Christ! "One died for all, therefore all have died… Therefore, if anyone is in Christ, he is a new creation. The old has passed away; behold, the new has come" (2 Corinthians 5:14, 17).

This is the most wonderful news, that our old selves in Adam have passed away and the new has come in Jesus Christ. This, we are told, is the one true baptism that saves us: Our baptism into Christ, which unites ourselves with Him, and takes us out of the old and places us into the new. And while discussing this, Peter clarifies himself, reminding us that it is *not* the ceremony of baptism that saves (which would be a work on our part). "Baptism, which corresponds to this, now saves you, *not* as a removal of dirt from the body…" (1 Peter 3:21). So it is not the ceremony of baptism that is the important part, but the spiritual reality of our baptism into Jesus Christ that matters.

"WE KNOW THAT OUR OLD SELF WAS CRUCIFIED…"

There is a wealth of truth found throughout Scripture. However, if we do not act on the truth we read in the Bible, it is of little use to us. Ultimately, truth not acted upon is lost. So when we read *these* truths in the book of Romans—that we've been baptized into Christ, along with His death and resurrection—we *must* respond to them in faith. How are we to go about doing this?

This passage gives several deliberate steps that every Christian must follow if they desire to appropriate their position in Christ. Understanding and practicing these things can radically transform our lives. However, as we study this passage, we must be careful to not reduce our life in Christ into a spiritual formula. While these are practical ways to respond to Romans 6 in faith, there is no quick path of spiritual growth. Seeking God and growing in grace are lifetime pursuits. Likewise, putting into practice Romans 6-8 will take a life of prayer and discipline in the Holy Spirit. A path of spiritual growth is woven into these verses; we would do well to reflect upon them while we study this passage:

- "We *know* that our old self was crucified with Him…" (Romans 6:6)
- "*Consider* yourselves dead to sin and alive to God in Christ Jesus…" (Romans 6:11)
- "*Present* yourselves to God as those who have been brought from death to life…" (Romans 6:13)

This, then, is the path we are to follow: Knowing ourselves to be crucified, considering (or reckoning) ourselves to be dead to sin and alive to God, and finally presenting ourselves to God as those who have been brought from death to life. Take great care to understand the significance of each step, pray about what is outlined in Romans 6, and then learn how to apply these truths. All the steps outlined here are connected to, and builds upon the previous ones, and are to be understood in order.

The apostle Paul tells us to begin with "knowing" ourselves to be crucified. "Do you not *know* that all of us who have been baptized into Christ Jesus were baptized into his death...We *know* that our old self was crucified with him" (Romans 6:3, 6). Unless we first know this to be true, we will not be able to proceed with considering and presenting ourselves to God. We must first know ourselves to have died with Christ! Now, the "knowing" that I am speaking of is not a mere agreement of the mind with facts. We need to *more* than just know something in our minds. The Holy Spirit must illuminate God's truth to us. This is very true. The apostle Paul, in writing to the Ephesians, tells them that he prays for them; that they would have the same sort of illumination of truth:

> I do not cease to give thanks for you, remembering you in my prayers, that the God of our Lord Jesus Christ, the Father of glory, may give you a spirit of wisdom and of revelation in the knowledge of him, having the eyes of your hearts enlightened. (Ephesians 1:16-18)

This is the kind of "knowing" needed here. When Simon Peter confessed that Jesus was the Christ in Caesarea Philippi, Jesus explained, "Blessed are you, Simon Bar-Jonah! For flesh and blood has not revealed this to you, but my Father who is in heaven" (Matthew 16:17). Spiritual insight comes supernaturally. We must have the eyes of our hearts opened to *know* that we have been crucified with Christ. We do not doubt that Jesus has been crucified; likewise, we must not doubt our own crucifixion. The same Bible speaks of both. The truth of our death with Jesus must reach the depths of ourselves; we must know it in the very marrow of our being. On the night He was betrayed, Jesus taught His disciples: "I still have many things to say to you, but you cannot bear them now. When the Spirit of truth comes, he will guide you into all the truth" (John 16:12-13). There are many things that God wants to teach us, but we cannot bear them on our own. We need strength in our inner being. In fact, any time we study the Scriptures the Holy Spirit must illuminate God's truth in order for us to comprehend it. Paul writes in another place:

> For who knows a person's thoughts except the spirit of that person, which is in him? So also no one comprehends the thoughts of God except the Spirit of God. Now we have received not the spirit of the world, but the Spirit who is from God, that we might understand things freely given us by God. And we impart this in words not taught by human wisdom but taught by the Spirit, interpreting spiritual truths to those who are spiritual. The natural person does not accept the things of the Spirit of God, for they are folly to him, and he is not able to understand them because they are spiritually discerned. The spiritual person judges all things, but is himself to be

> judged by no one. "For who has understood the mind of the Lord so as to instruct Him?" But we have the mind of Christ. (1 Corinthians 2:14-16)

Spiritual truth is spiritually discerned. No one can understand the thoughts of God except for the Spirit of God. That is one of the ministries of the Holy Spirit. He illuminates God's truth to us. This is not just correct knowledge, but a particular kind of understanding, imparted *directly* by the Holy Spirit where He gives us a sense of excellence of the truth written in the Bible. This is certainly true in the matter of knowing ourselves to be crucified with Christ. We must have the eyes of our heart opened to this matter, piercing our souls and giving us a sense of divine reality.

I think it is so beautiful here when the Bible tells us that "we have the mind of Christ." Jesus is our wise and constant Rabbi. He wants to come and walk with us and teach us spiritual truth; all through the presence of the Holy Spirit. No longer does the Messiah merely walk along the shorelines of the Sea of Galilee or through the streets of Jerusalem, now He treads upon city sidewalks and college campuses. He warmly invites each of us to sit as His feet and to learn spiritual things from Him. And He will teach us to *know* ourselves to have been crucified. He will so convince the mind, showing "that one died for all, therefore all have died" (2 Corinthians 5:14). Yes, Jesus Christ—through the agency of the Holy Spirit—will teach us great spiritual truth, certainly this truth as well, if we would only ask Him.

The importance of knowing should not surprise us,

for in the same way our second birth began by a different kind of knowing. Specifically, we knew that Jesus had come, and that He had died for our sins and rose from the dead, and that if we would ask for forgiveness and put our faith in Christ alone that we would be saved. We *knew* this. If we had not first known these things to be true, we would have never put our faith in the Messiah. We would have never become Christians. It is written, "Faith comes by hearing, and hearing through the word of Christ" (Romans 10:17). In the very same way, we must first *know* ourselves to have died with Jesus. "Do you not know that all of us who have been baptized into Christ Jesus were baptized into his death?" (Romans 6:3). We need to hear the Bible well on this matter.

And yet, as you read these words right now, you may not *feel* that you have been crucified—instead, you may feel that your identity is still dictated by Adam. Perhaps you don't see the reality of your death with Jesus to be working its way out in your experience. But we must take God at His word. We must fully believe ourselves to have been crucified because *God tells us it is so.* Our crucifixion is once-for-all. It has already been done to us, in the historical death of Christ, and won't ever be undone. When we wanted to put our faith in the Lord Jesus for our salvation, we did not ask Him to come and die for our sins. No, we *knew* that He had already done this. We simply trusted Him by faith and thanked the Savior for His sacrifice. Likewise, it would be pointless to ask God to crucify us again, for He has already done it. We must trust Scripture and rest in its truth, regardless of our shifting feelings. The same Bible that tells us that Jesus was crucified also tells us that *we* were crucified with Him. "I have been crucified with Christ. It is no longer I who live, but Christ who lives in me. And the life I now live in the flesh I live by faith in the Son of God, who loved me and gave himself for me" (Galatians 2:20). Why should we believe in one and not the other? We must *know* ourselves to have died with Christ, and God will begin to radically transform our lives because of this knowledge, if we then, after knowing, do this: Reckon ourselves to be dead to sin and then finally present ourselves to God as instruments of righteousness.

"CONSIDER YOURSELVES DEAD TO SIN…"

After the Holy Spirit has given us eyes to see, having "known" ourselves to be crucified with Jesus, we must follow the next step: "considering" (or "reckoning," as many translations say). The apostle Paul writes:

> So you also must consider yourselves dead to sin and alive to God in Christ Jesus. (Romans 6:11)

As Christians we are called to *reckon* (or consider) ourselves to be dead to sin and alive to God in Jesus Christ. I cannot overemphasize how important it is to first *know*, or else our reckoning will useless. Often, there is too much emphasis on first reckoning truth in order to know. This is an error, and will only lead to frustration and failure.

And what is it that we are reckoning? *We are reckoning that because we have died with Jesus Christ, we are likewise dead to sin.* Specifically, that we have been crucified with Jesus for a reason, "in order that the body of sin might be *brought to nothing*, so that we would no longer be enslaved to sin" (Romans 6:6). And what does it mean to be "dead" to sin? Or, put another way, what does it mean for "the body of sin to be brought to nothing?" *The phrase "brought to nothing" comes from a root word in the Greek that means "inactive" or "unemployed."*

Jesus told a parable in Matthew 20:1-16 that described what the kingdom of heaven is like. In the parable Jesus talked about a master who owned a vineyard. On a certain day the master kept going out into the streets to find workers who were *idle*, so that he could hire them to work in his vineyard for the day. The word that has been translated into "idle" in the parable comes from the same root word of the phrase "brought to nothing." The idea here is that while sin *was* our old master, when Christ was made sin (2 Corinthian 5:21) and we died with Him, we became unemployed. We *used* to be slaves to sin in Adam, and sin turned the members of our bodies into instruments of unrighteousness. But now we have been set free from sin in Christ. Before we had no choice in the matter. We were slaves to sin. Sin was our master, and we could not keep from sinning. The Scriptures tell us of our old life:

> And you were dead in the trespasses and sins in which you once walked, following the prince of the power of the air, the spirit that is now at work in the sons of disobedience—among whom we all once lived in the passions of our flesh, carrying out the desires of the body and the mind,

and were by nature children of wrath, like
the rest of mankind. (Ephesians 2:1-3)

Yet, we were united with Jesus in His death, and are no longer enslaved to our old master, "For one who has died has been set free from sin" (Romans 6:7). However, we will *always* choose to be a slave to sin again if we do not practice the next exhortation in Romans: presenting ourselves to God.

For quite some time, I made a mistake when reading this passage. When I read to "consider yourselves dead to sin" (Romans 6:11), I felt it meant to "think of yourselves *as if* you are dead to sin." The error with this thinking is that it deceptively implies the *opposite* of what it should. It is as if the mind is saying, "Look at yourself *as if* you are dead to sin, but you're *really* not dead to sin." It would be the same as if a father said to his son, "I think of you *as if* you are my son." The son would think his father to be out of his right mind. No, the father would say, "You are my son." The phrase "as if," although it sounds nice, undermines the very meaning itself. Likewise, thinking of yourself *as if* you were dead to sin, as nice as it might sound, undermines what the passage is teaching—that we have died with Jesus and thus are no longer enslaved to sin.

Therefore, we must reckon ourselves to be dead to sin and alive to God in Christ Jesus, *because it is the truth.* God's word only declares truth and life, and He only asks us to reckon things to be true because they *are* true. We do not reckon ourselves to be dead to sin in order to die, we reckon ourselves to be dead to sin because we are *already* dead. If we have been crucified with Christ, then we are dead. Failure to know and reckon this truth will not make it untrue. Likewise, if we are *not* dead, no amount of reckoning will make us dead. We reckon ourselves to be dead because we are dead.

Let's speak of what the word "reckoning" means. Then we shall understand what it means to reckon ourselves to be dead to sin. Many errors will be avoided if we understand the implications of "considering" or "reckoning," as well as what it doesn't mean. The word in the original Greek carries with it the idea of accounting or bookkeeping. It will help us greatly to see this. We should read these verses carefully, and then notice their meaning:

> We know that our old self was crucified with him in order that the body of sin might be brought to nothing, so that we would no longer be enslaved to sin. For one who has died has been set free from sin. Now if we have died with Christ, we believe that we will also live with him. We know that Christ being raised from the dead will never die again; death no longer has dominion over him. For the death he died he died to sin, once for all, but the life he lives he lives to God. So you also must consider yourselves dead to sin and alive to God in Christ Jesus. (Romans 6:6-11)

So, in order to "reckon" or "consider" we must do the following: We must be like careful accountants here, checking our books and doing the math so that we can correctly reckon the truth. We are told that the death Jesus died He died to sin, and that the life He lives He lives to God. We are also told that we died with Christ and that we also live with Him. Now we must do the math: Jesus died to sin, and Jesus lives to God (Romans 6:10). Likewise, we died with Jesus and we live with Jesus (Romans 6:8). This means—by virtue of our co-death and co-resurrection with Christ—we *too* have died to sin and are now alive to God in Christ Jesus (Romans 6:11). Because Christ was crucified and died to sin, and we were baptized into Him, we also died to sin. This is the truth we are to consider. We are now to live as people who have died and risen again, no longer to be enslaved to the power of sin.

The question immediately arises: *If we have died to sin, then why do we still sin?* This is because the power of sin still remains in our bodies, ready once again to take captive our members as instruments of unrighteousness. We are *not* told that the power of sin has been eradicated from our lives. To reckon this would be a grave mistake. While the penalty of our sins has been paid for by the blood of the Lamb, sin as a principle has not been removed. John writes in one of his epistles, "If we say we have no sin, we deceive ourselves, and the truth is not in us" (1 John 1:8). Let's not deceive ourselves. The sin that clings so closely is still real and present in the life of the Christian, and if we reckon it to be gone we will get ourselves into trouble. The apostle pleads with us: "Let not sin therefore reign in your mortal bodies, to make you obey their passions" (Romans 6:12).

And when should a Christian "consider?" I've found in my own life that at the very moment of temptation I must bring into consideration that I am dead to sin. I have become unemployed. Any time the power of sin is working to take captive the members of my body, I must pause and consider: *I have died to sin. Sin is no longer my master. I am no slave; now I have a choice.* Paul's words ring ever true: "No temptation has overtaken you that is not common to man. God is faithful, and he will not let you be tempted beyond your ability; but with the temptation he will also provide the way of escape, that you may be able to endure it" (1 Corinthians 10:13). As new creations in Christ, we do not have to succumb to temptation, but can find victories in our lives. There will be struggle, yes, there will often be failures. And while we will never be perfect in this life, we can experience life, peace, and even freedom in the Spirit.

This, consequently, is what we are told to reckon: While sin was our old master, when we died with Jesus we became "unemployed." We no longer must be slaves to sin. This is great news indeed! Christ died to sin, and lives to God, and by being joined with Him, we died to sin and live to God. Now, as new creatures in Christ, we are given an important choice: Will we continue being slaves to sin? Or will we choose to present our newly "unemployed" bodies to God as instruments of righteousness?

"PRESENT YOURSELVES TO GOD…"

The apostle Paul clearly intends for these considerations to lead to a *practical* deliverance from sin: "What shall we say then? Are we to continue in sin that grace may abound? *By no means*! How can we who died to sin still live in it?" (Romans 6:1-2) Paul finds it unthinkable that a Christian—who has died to sin—can still habitually live in it. We have died with Jesus, and rose with Him, and now are new creatures in Christ. Sin is no longer our master.

So now that we reckon that the members of our bodies are "unemployed" or "idle," we now *must* make a choice. We will not remain idle indefinitely. Paul continues:

> Let not sin therefore reign in your mortal bodies, to make you obey their passions. Do not present your members to sin as instruments for unrighteousness, but present yourselves to God as those who have been brought from death to life, and your members to God as instruments for righteousness. (Romans 6:12-13)

This is what the Scripture challenges us with: After we have died with Christ and are no longer slaves to sin, will we now present ourselves to our new master, God, as instruments for His righteousness? Or will we try to remain idle a little while longer and allow our old master, sin, to take captive the members of our bodies as instruments of unrighteousness? *We must make a choice.* You see, humans are slaves by nature. Human beings were made to be mastered. At any moment we are either going to present ourselves to God, as those who have risen from the dead with Jesus, or we are going to, *by default*, yield our bodies to sin as instruments of unrighteousness. There is no middle ground. At any moment we are again becoming slaves of sin, or we are becoming slaves of God. This is not a fallacy; it is reality as it is presented in Romans 6. The Bible tells us that whichever master we present ourselves to, we *will* become their slave:

> Do you not know that if you present yourselves to anyone as obedient slaves, *you are slaves of the one whom you obey*, either of sin, which leads to death, or of obedience, which leads to righteousness? (Romans 6:16)

Jesus once declared, "Truly, truly, I say to you, everyone who commits sin is a slave to sin" (John 8:34). Any time we sin, it is because we have presented our members to the power of sin and thus have become its obedient slave.

Finally, we are told twice in this chapter that when we become slaves of sin, what it leads to is *death* (Romans 6:16, 6:21). What is death? It is not referring to the funeral at the end of your life. That is not the kind of death mentioned here. We all have sinned many times without physically dying. Paul is writing here about a *quality* of death. Death, really, is the absence of life. When paramedics are called to an emergency, and they come upon a body, they do not check for signs of death. They instead look for signs of life—breathing, a heartbeat, and so forth. Once it is determined that those signs of life are *missing*, the body is declared dead. We have talked before about walking in the light and having fellowship with God. We were careful to mention that darkness was the *absence* of light. Wherever light is missing, there is darkness. The same is true here of life and death. Death is the absence of life. Jesus said that He came that we may have life, and have it abundantly (John 10:10). What do we call it when we are *not* experiencing that quality of life? Death! We are given a picture of what life in Jesus Christ is like in Galatians:

> The fruit of the Spirit is love, joy, peace, patience, kindness, goodness, faithfulness, gentleness, self-control... (Galatians 5:22, 23)

So if all those wonderful qualities are *life*, and are part of an abundant life in Christ, what does death look like? Well, just the opposite:

> Now the works of the flesh are evident: Sexual immorality, impurity, sensuality, idolatry, sorcery, enmity, strife, jealousy, fits of anger, rivalries, dissensions, divisions, envy, drunkenness, orgies, and things like these. (Galatians 5: 19-21)

The difference between presenting ourselves to God and presenting ourselves to sin is the difference between life and death. We must feel the weight of these words, and always be presenting ourselves to God. "But now that you have been set free from sin and have become slaves of God, the fruit you get leads to sanctification and its end, eternal life" (Romans 6:22). The eternal life mentioned here doesn't merely refer to life after death (although it certainly includes that). It is also concerned with a *quality* of life; our life in Christ, the vigor and strength of our spirituality.

The choice is clear. Do we want to be slaves to sin, which derives its power ultimately from Satan? Of course not. Yet we know that at any moment, we are *going* to be a slave, whether by choice or by force. It is our nature. Those who are slaves to God shall reap a reward of righteousness.

Often times God presents us with heavenly principles that seems upside down to us: The first shall be last, the least shall be greatest, in order to save our lives we must lose them, and so on. Here is another principle: If we would like to be free, we must become a slave to Jesus. We must *know* ourselves to be crucified, *reckon* ourselves to be dead to sin and no longer its slave, and finally *present* ourselves to God are those who have risen from the dead. Knowing, reckoning, and presenting—these are things to grasp and practice in light of our death with Jesus. This is not all there is to Christianity, and we must be careful to not reduce spirituality to formulas, but this knowledge will give us a good base for exploring true spirituality in Jesus Christ.

CHAPTER 04 – THE INDWELLING LIFE OF CHRIST

Christ in you, the hope of glory. (Colossians 1:27)

CHRIST: THE LAST ADAM, THE SECOND MAN

Listen:

We were not crucified with Christ as an end to itself. While in the Christian life there are often negatives—the biggest negative in history being the cross of Jesus—it always moves on to a positive. After even the darkest night, the sun rises in the morning. Revisiting the passage in Romans 6, the Scriptures explain the divine purpose for our death with Jesus:

> We were buried therefore with him by baptism into death, *in order that*, just as Christ was raised from the dead by the glory of the Father, we too might walk in newness of life. (Romans 6:4)

We were crucified not only to end our old lives in Adam, but so that we would *rise from the dead with Jesus*, that "we too might walk in newness of life." The old life was done away with at the cross, the new life walked out of the tomb.

Paul continues, "For if we have been united with him in a death like his, we shall *certainly* be united with him in a resurrection like his" (Romans 6:5). Just as the Holy Spirit has pierced our souls with knowing our death with the Savior, now must our eyes be opened to the significance of resurrection; for as certainly as we died with Jesus Christ, we also rose from the dead with Him.

Christ is given two fantastic titles in 1 Corinthians 15. First, Jesus is called "the last Adam" (1 Corinthians 15:45). This means that everything that was of Adam was done away with in the death of Jesus. By the cross of Christ, we were cut off from our old lives in Adam—thus Jesus is the last Adam. The slavery to sin that was planted in the Garden of Eden was brought to nothing at Golgotha. Yet also in this passage Christ is given a second title: He is the "second man" (1 Corinthians 15:47). As the second man, Jesus has in effect started a new race of people. Members of this new race are not born of Adam, as the first race was. These people have been born of God:

> But to all who did receive him, who believed in his name, he gave the right to become children of God, who were born, not of blood nor of the will of the flesh nor of the will of man, but of God. (John 1:12-13)

After the first man fell, he was merely a man of dust. He was a man of dirt and was not spiritual. We all bore his image. The second man—Jesus—was from heaven. His resurrection brings new life, spiritual life, and Christians bear His image. This brings us to an important question: What does it mean to have been born of God?

THE NATURE OF HUMANITY

To understand the new spiritual birth, we must again return to the creation account in Genesis. The book of Romans explains the fall in the garden, which constituted all of Adam's offspring as sinners, and apart from Jesus all stand condemned and face God's judgment. Yet, we missed an important piece in the puzzle. We have not explained what it means when Genesis proclaims that God created male and female in His own image (Genesis 1:26-27). And to understand this, we must briefly discuss the nature of our humanity.

In his first letter to the Thessalonians, Paul mentions—although without discussion or explanation—a threefold nature to our humanity:

> Now may the God of peace himself sanctify you completely, and may your whole spirit and soul and body be kept blameless at the coming of our Lord Jesus Christ. (1 Thessalonians 5:23)

Each person consists of three integrated parts: Body, soul, and spirit. Although there are three distinct "pieces" that each human consist of, there is still a unity in them, for they all function together to make a whole being.

The body is the physical aspect of our being, allowing us to interact with the material world. Our bodies are the vehicles here on earth that houses the soul and spirit. The Lord made Adam out of dust and gave him a body (Genesis 2:7). There is nothing wrong or lesser in the physical aspect of our being as many Greeks theorized, for it was God's design. In creation, God declared the physical world He had made to be *good*. Jesus came into the physical world at the incarnation and gained a body just like the rest of humanity, "And the Word became flesh and dwelt among us" (John 1:14). Likewise, Jesus' physical resurrection is our only hope for our own resurrection after death (1 Corinthians 15:17-19). The apostle Paul refers to our bodies as an *earthly tent*, our dwelling while we are here on earth until the time comes for our heavenly dwelling, a building from God:

> For we know that if the tent, which is our earthly home, is destroyed, we have a building from God, a house not made with hands, eternal in the heavens. For in this tent we groan, longing to put on our heavenly dwelling, if indeed by putting it on we may not be found naked. For while we are still in this tent, we groan, being burdened—not that we would be unclothed, but that we would be further clothed, so that what is mortal may be swallowed up by life. (1 Corinthians 5:1-4)

This notion of our bodies as an earthly tent is helpful, for when we read that "the Word became flesh and dwelt among us" (John 1:14), the word *dwelt* speaks of the ancient tabernacle, when God dwelt among His people in a literal tent. Jesus, in the incarnation, donned *His* earthly tent, a body of flesh, and we read that He "tabernacled" among us.

Just as there are three parts to our humanity, there are three aspects to our souls as well. The soul consists of mind, will, and emotion. The mind is for thinking, the will is for choosing, and emotions are for feeling. All three of these are closely in relation and affect one another. For example, the thoughts we have in our minds will influence our emotions, both of which in turn can radically affect the decisions we make via the faculty of our wills.

The soul was created for God. When man fell, the soul became a slave to the devil and his world system (John 8:34, 2 Corinthians 4:4, Revelation 18:13). The mind was created for knowing God, but instead people exchange the truth about God for a lie. The emotions were created for loving Him and delighting in His goodness, but now men love darkness rather than the light. And the while the will was created for choosing God, humanity now chooses evil.

Having a soul is *not* what makes us in the image of God, for even the animals have souls. Animals think with their minds, and feel with their emotions, and use their wills to make decisions, just as humans do. I would be terrified to face the anger (emotion) of a mother grizzly bear when it understands (mind) that I am standing between she and her cubs, and chooses (will) to charge me. All of those experiences lie in the realm in the soul, even in animals. These functions, however, are largely based upon animal instinct.

Today there is not much distinction made between the soul and spirit. Even though in common langue the two words are often used interchangeably, the Scriptures distinguish between the two:

> For the word of God is living and active, sharper than any two-edged sword, piercing to *the division of soul and of spirit*, of joints and of marrow, and discerning the thoughts and intentions of the heart. (Hebrews 2:12)

The Bible *does* make a distinction between the soul and spirit. And what is spirit in man? It is the one aspect of humanity that sets them apart from the rest of creation. The human spirit is the part of man's being that allows him to know and to relate to God. God's Spirit was meant to dwell within man's spirit, for we are told, "He who is joined to the Lord becomes one spirit with him" (1 Corinthians 6:17). Through this connection with man, God would display His image in humanity. God's Spirit would captivate the human soul; conforming mind, will, and emotion to true righteousness and holiness. This is what it means for man to have been made in the image of God. By His presence within the human spirit, the invisible Creator would then be able to display *His* quality of life within humans.

When Adam and Eve were in Eden, God gave them instructions as to what fruit they could eat and which were forbidden: "And the Lord God commanded the man, saying, 'You may surely eat of every tree of the garden, but of the tree of the knowledge of good and evil you shall not eat, for in the day that you eat of it you shall surely *die*'" (Genesis 2:16-17). However, our first parents *did* eat of the tree of the knowledge of good and evil. Yet they did not die physically on the day they ate the fruit. Adam lived to an astonishing age of 930 years before death finally claimed him. Many explain that the death Adam and Eve experienced in Eden was only a spiritual death. This is partly true—the first humans *did* die spiritually that day. And yet it is vital to understand that there was a physical aspect to their death as well. In the day Adam and Eve ate the forbidden fruit, they became mortal. Their bodies became subject to decay and corruption—all of which would culminate in death. The judgment of the Almighty came to them, saying, "For you are dust, and to dust you shall return" (Genesis 3:19).

Yet there was also a *different* kind of death in the garden. It was a spiritual death. In the moment that Adam sinned in Eden, the one holy God withdrew His Spirit from man's spirit. Consequently, man has been left spiritually dead, "alienated from the life of God" (Ephesians 4:18). This is yet another part of our heritage in Adam, bearing his likeness.

GLORY

There is a thread running through the Scriptures centered on the idea of *glory*. For instance, when the Lord created mankind, He did so for *His* glory (Isaiah 43:7). Likewise, King David declared of God's act in creating man:

> What is man that you are mindful of him,
> and the son of man that you care for him?
> Yet you have made him a little lower than
> the heavenly beings and *crowned him with*
> *glory* and honor. (Psalm 8:4-5)

Human beings were created "crowned with glory." What is glory? Glory is almost exclusively associated with the presence of the Lord. God is the most glorious being. Whenever a manifestation of God's presence is recorded in Scripture, it is written that whoever was there saw the glory of the Lord (Exodus 40:34-35, Ezekiel 43:1-5). When the Ark of the Covenant was captured by the Philistines in 1 Samuel 4, the people lamented, "The glory has departed from Israel, for the ark of God has been captured" (1 Samuel 4:22). While Moses was on Mount Sinai, he pleaded with God to show him His glory—the very manifestation of God's presence (Exodus 33:18-20). Likewise, the prophet Ezekiel received this vision of God:

> Seated above the likeness of a throne was
> a likeness with a human appearance. And
> upward from what had the appearance of
> his waist I saw as it were gleaming metal,
> like the appearance of fire enclosed all
> around. And downward from what had
> the appearance of his waist I saw as it
> were the appearance of fire, and there was
> brightness around him. Like the
> appearance of the bow that is in the cloud

> on the day of rain, so was the appearance
> of the brightness all around. *Such was the*
> *appearance of the likeness of the glory of the*
> *Lord.* And when I saw it, I fell on my
> face. (Ezekiel 1:26-28)

Glory denotes the manifestation of God's presence. Thus the glory human beings were crowned with was a *derived* glory, one that came from having the life of God dwell within them. This glory is far greater than anything we could ever hope to attain to in our own best efforts. This is man in his innocence, as the Lord originally created him—crowned with glory. Human beings were to reflect God's glory as image-bearers of God. However, we are told this when humanity fell in the garden:

> For all have sinned and *fall short of the glory*
> *of God.* (Romans 3:23)

All of humanity has fallen short of the glory of God because of unrighteousness. A holy God cannot allow His presence to dwell within wickedness. God is light, in Him is no darkness at all (1 John 1:5). When Moses pleaded with the Lord to dwell with Israel, God declared, "Say to the people of Israel, 'You are a stiff-necked people; for if for a single moment I should go up among you, I would consume you'" (Exodus 33:5). Desiring God to dwell within such close proximity to a sinful people was a dangerous thing. The tabernacle solved this problem. The tabernacle was to keep a holy God from destroying all of Israel! The same is true of sinners. Because humanity has fallen short of the glory of God, the Lord's spirit has cleaved itself from man's spirit. When mankind was constituted as sinners in Eden, that derived glory was lost. Humanity was made to reflect the glory of God, but instead became sinners, murderers, not loving goodness and righteousness, sexually immoral, and thieves.

And what did Christ achieve when He died for our sins, was buried, and rose from the dead on the third day? Not only did Jesus justify and redeem us by His blood, but the writer of Hebrews explains that Jesus came in order to bring *"many sons to glory"* (Hebrews 2:10). Part of Christ's work is to restore His people to glory, the glory that the Father crowned us with at creation, which was forfeited because of sin and unrighteousness. And what is the glory that Jesus came to restore? The apostle Paul writes in his letter to the Colossians of a great mystery, one that was hidden throughout the ages, but was his privilege to reveal:

> I became a minister according to the stewardship from God that was given to me for you, to make the word of God fully known, the mystery hidden for ages and generations but now revealed to his saints. To them God chose to make known how great among the Gentiles are the riches of the glory of this mystery, which is *Christ in you, the hope of glory.* (Colossians 1:25-27)

This is the revealed mystery: God in Jesus Christ has once again come to live in the temple of the human heart, and the glory of the Lord is being formed in His new creation. "He who is joined to the Lord becomes one spirit with him… Do you not know that your body is a temple of the Holy Spirit within you, whom you have from God?" (1 Corinthians 6:17, 19). Likewise, Jesus spoke of the Spirit, "The Spirit of truth… You know him, for he dwells with you and will be in you" (John 14:17). This is indeed most wonderful news, that the Lord has once again united His Spirit with ours. We shall explore the deep implications of this truth, that every Christian can claim that it is "Christ who lives in me" (Galatians 2:20). We are indeed the body of Christ.

When God made Adam in Genesis, He pushed together a little pile of dust and breathed life into it. In doing this, Adam became a living being. Paul revisits this idea in 1 Corinthians 15, but contrasts it with the life that *Jesus* imparts:

> Thus it is written, "The first man Adam became a living being"; the last Adam became a life-giving spirit. (1 Corinthians 15:45)

Jesus Christ; the last Adam, the second man, became a life-giving spirit.

How did Jesus impart new spiritual life to us? *It was by our unity with Him in His resurrection.* The Scriptures declare that God "made us alive together with Christ" (Ephesians 2:5). This is the newness of life that we may walk in: The very life of Jesus, living inside of us, making all things new by imparting to us His life. I can think of nothing as exciting as the life of Jesus Christ being manifest inside of a person who has crossed from death to life!

"YOU MUST BE BORN AGAIN…"

Under the secret cover of night, Nicodemus, a Pharisee and a ruler of the Jews, came to speak with Jesus. Nicodemus had heard of the many signs that Christ had performed, and he knew that Jesus was a teacher sent from God (John 3:1-2). It is in this conversation that the Teacher tells Nicodemus, "Truly, truly, I say to you, unless one is born again he cannot see the kingdom of God" (John 3:3). Nicodemus did not understand the words Jesus had spoken. He asked, how could a man enter *again* into his mother's womb to be reborn? But Christ clarified what He meant:

> "Truly, truly, I say to you, unless one is born of water and the Spirit, he cannot enter the kingdom of God. That which is born of the flesh is flesh, and that which is born of the Spirit is spirit." (John 3:5-6)

Jesus declared that unless a person has a *second* birth they cannot enter the kingdom of God. Everyone that would enter into Christ's kingdom must have a second birth, a spiritual birth. Without being born again we will not even see the kingdom. And from this passage we understand that this quality of life cannot come naturally, for "that which is born of the flesh is flesh" (John 3:6). The second birth must come by supernatural means, for "that which is born of the Spirit is spirit" (John 3:6). We must be born of the Spirit of God to enter Christ's kingdom. Jesus explained to Nicodemus that it was for this very reason that He came:

"No one has ascended into heaven except he who descended from heaven, the Son of Man. And as Moses lifted up the serpent in the wilderness, so must the Son of Man be lifted up, that whoever believes in him may have eternal life. For God so loved the world, that he gave his only Son, that whoever believes in him should not perish but have eternal life." (John 3:13-15)

Here Christ explains how these things can be: That He would be crucified for our sins, and "so must the Son of Man be lifted up," so to all who believe in Him are granted life from the second birth. Everyone who receives Jesus has been born of God (John 1:12-13). That is their birthright. Every person who believes in the name of "He who descended from heaven" has life. The apostle Paul made a similar statement when he argues for the resurrection from the dead:

As was the man of dust, so also are those who are of the dust, and as is the man of heaven, so also are those who are of heaven. Just as we have borne the image of the man of dust, we shall also bear the image of the man of heaven. (1 Corinthians 15:48-49)

We used to be mere men of dust—spiritually dead, alienated from the life of God—bearing the image of the first man of dust, Adam. But now we are men of heaven;

now we bear the image of the Man of heaven—the very life of Jesus Christ!

Peter writes concerning the resurrection, that God "has caused us to be born again to a living hope through the resurrection of Jesus Christ from the dead" (1 Peter 1:3). United in His resurrection, we have crossed from death to life. We have been born a second time with Christ who is our life (Colossians 3:4).

I think it is beautiful that we've been "born again to a living hope." We've been made alive with Christ, and we possess a *living hope* because Jesus rose from the dead and *He is our hope* (1 Timothy 1:1). Tell me, right now as you are reading this: Is Jesus *your* living hope? My sincere prayer is that He is. His life is dwelling inside of you. The thought of Jesus as our living hope will guard our minds like a helmet, like a beautiful song. Jesus Christ *is* hope.

It was through our unity with Christ in His resurrection that God has imparted to us new spiritual life—the very life of Jesus. There is a powerful passage in Ephesians that is before us now. It is a passage I often return to for meditation and prayer:

> For this reason, because I have heard of your faith in the Lord Jesus and your love toward all the saints, I do not cease to give thanks for you, remembering you in my prayers, that the God of our Lord Jesus Christ, the Father of glory, may give you a spirit of wisdom and of revelation in the knowledge of him, having the eyes of your hearts enlightened, that you may know what is the hope to which he has

called you, what are the riches of his
glorious inheritance in the saints, and
what is the immeasurable greatness of his
power toward us who believe, according
to the working of his great might that he
worked in Christ when He raised him
from the dead and seated him at his right
hand in the heavenly places. (Ephesians
1:15-20)

Paul had a fondness of heart for the church in Ephesus.
He was continually thankful for them, because of their
faith in Jesus and love for one another. He never ceased
to pray for them, that the Spirit might illuminate truth to
them, that the eyes of their hearts might be opened. And
what *specifically* does he pray for? He prays that they "may
know what is the *hope to which he has called you*, what are the
riches of his glorious inheritance in the saints, and what *is the
immeasurable greatness of his power* toward us who believe."
(Ephesians 1:18-19). Paul prays for them to know three
important things; all of which we ought to know as well:

- The *hope* to which He has called us
- The riches of His *glorious inheritance* in the
  saints
- The immeasurable greatness of His *power*
  toward us who believe

What is the hope to which God has called Christians?
Well, it is the hope that we have discussed: That Christ
rose from the dead in accordance with the Scriptures. And
because of Christ's historical, physical resurrection, and
our being united with Him in it, that we have crossed from

death to life. We have been born again. It is what Job spoke of in his suffering: "For I know that my Redeemer lives, and at the last he will stand upon the earth. And after my skin has been destroyed, yet in my flesh I shall see God" (Job 19:25-26). We know that we possess life, because Jesus rose from the dead. Because He lives, we also shall live. This is our hope. Jesus Christ is our living hope.

What is His glorious inheritance in the saints? It is the same glory we have talked at length about: Christ in us, the hope of glory. The glory forfeited in Eden is being renewed day by day as we are being conformed to Christ's image, as we look to things eternal.

And finally, what is the immeasurable greatness of power that God has toward those who believe? Paul explains that this power, which is so infinite to conceive, is the same power "that he worked in Christ when he raised him from the dead and seated him at his right hand in the heavenly places" (Ephesians 1:20). *The power that the Lord has towards us who believe is the power that the Father worked to raise Jesus Christ from the dead.* This is very significant because of what Paul later writes:

> But God, being rich in mercy, because of the great love with which he loved us, even when we were dead in our trespasses, made us alive together with Christ—by grace you have been saved—and raised us up with him and seated us with him in the heavenly places in Christ Jesus. (Ephesians 2:4-6)

It is this *same power*, the one that God worked in Christ in the resurrection, which He has also worked in *us*.

We have been raised *with* Jesus—"made alive *together* with Christ!"—and just as the Son was seated in the heavenly places, we are also seated with Him. It is for this very reason that Jesus could assure His disciples: "I will not leave you as orphans; I will come to you. Yet a little while and the world will see me no more, but you will see me. *Because I live, you also will live.* In that day you will know that I am in my Father, and you in me, and I in you" (John 14:18-20). Jesus lives, and we also live. We are in Christ, yes, and His life is in us. We are not orphans; we are children of God. Christ has truly brought many sons to glory! And we see that we are alive, because Jesus is alive and living in us.

I pray that the Holy Spirit opens the eyes of your heart too, that you will know the living hope you possess in Jesus, the glory Christ is restoring in your life, and the power the Father has toward all whom believe. The truth of our death and second birth with Jesus is not limited to only a few passages in Scripture, but is a glorious fact that rings throughout the entire Bible:

> We were buried therefore with him by baptism into death, in order that, just as Christ was raised from the dead by the glory of the Father, we too might walk in newness of life. (Romans 6:4)

> For as in Adam all die, so also in Christ shall all be made alive. (1 Corinthians 15:22)

Therefore, if anyone is in Christ, he is a new creation. The old has passed away; behold, the new has come. (2 Corinthians 5:17)

You were also raised with him through faith in the powerful working of God, who raised him from the dead. And you, who were dead in your trespasses and the uncircumcision of your flesh, God made alive together with him. (Colossians 2:12-13)

TO LIVE IS CHRIST

We have been made alive with Jesus. Now we must ask ourselves the vital question: What are we to do with this truth? How are we to respond to it in faith? The first thing to understand is that because of the spiritual birth, *Christ is now our life*. "For you have died, and your life is hidden with Christ in God. When Christ who is your life appears, then you also will appear with Him in glory" (Colossians 3:3-4).

From this we understand that only Jesus can live the Christian life, for the simple fact that He *is* the Christian life. The more we detach ourselves from Jesus as our life and strength, the further from true spirituality we shall drift. There is nothing as vile as a professing Christian who does not know Christ. Apart from the living person of Jesus there is no spiritual reality, only hypocrisy and dead religion. And yet there is nothing that is as vibrant and powerful as a person living in close communion with Jesus.

Once I began to learn about the resurrection in my own life, that Jesus is living inside of me, and about my life in Christ, that Jesus is my wisdom and righteousness and sanctification and redemption (1 Corinthians 1:30), my spiritual life really began to *thrive*. For the first time, the Bible began to make sense to me. Times of prayer and meditation on the Scriptures took new depth and meaning, because *He* was there. I was discovering the indispensable presence of Jesus in my life. And yet I was not perfect. I still had failures and hardships. I still do. But I began to understand what Paul meant when he wrote, "to live is Christ" (Philippians 1:21).

With Jesus living inside of us, we can now know Him in a real and intimate way. Our Savior prayed for each one of us, "And this is eternal life, that they know you the only true God, and Jesus Christ whom you have sent" (John 17:3). Life comes in knowing God, and knowing Him in the person of Jesus Christ.

The apostle John also writes in one of his epistles: "And this is the testimony, that God gave us eternal life, and this life is in his Son. Whoever has the Son has life; whoever does not have the Son of God does not have life" (1 John 5:11-12). Eternal life is found in Christ alone. And if we desire to experience the life that Jesus spoke of, we must find it in a living, vital fellowship with Him. He invites us to come to Him, and to talk with Him, and find rest in Him. The nearer we draw to Jesus Christ, who is our life, the more we will find the deepest needs of the human heart are satisfied in Him.

"AS THOSE WHO HAVE BEEN BROUGHT FROM DEATH TO LIFE…"

We understand the proper response to our being baptized into Christ's death and resurrection: to know ourselves to be crucified with Jesus, to consider ourselves to be dead to sin, and finally to present ourselves to God as instruments of righteousness.

Now, when we are told to present ourselves to God, we are told to do so in a certain manner: "Present yourselves to God *as those who have been brought from death to life*, and your members to God as instruments of righteousness" (Romans 6:13). This, then, is the key to presenting: We are to present ourselves to the Father as *people who have risen from the dead*, as those who have been brought to a new spiritual life in Christ. This is significant, because now we shall understand the outworking of our presenting.

The Spirit of God now dwells again within the human spirit, for, "He who is joined to the Lord becomes *one spirit with Him*" (1 Corinthians 6:17). When we present ourselves to God, we are in effect saying, "Here I am! Have all of me!" and we allow God to have full access to the human soul—mind, will, and emotions. He will then express *His* life in us, in "true righteousness and holiness" (Ephesians 4:24). He will work to conform us to the image of Christ. We will know God with our minds, for we have the mind of Christ (1 Corinthians 2:16). We shall love God and others with our emotions as we ought, for the love of Christ guides us (2 Corinthians 5:14-15). And we will learn to say "no" to ourselves and "yes" to God, for He is even changing our very will (Philippians 2:13).

We are likewise told that when we died with Christ and rose with Him, that we were made new creations in Him:

> For the love of Christ controls us, because we have concluded this: that one died for all, therefore all have died; and he died for all, that those who live might no longer live for themselves but for him who for their sake died and was raised... Therefore, if anyone is in Christ, he is a new creation. The old has passed away; behold, the new has come. (1 Corinthians 5:14-15, 17)

And yet there is an outworking of *this* precious truth as well. We are continually exhorted to *put on* the new self:

> Put off your old self, which belongs to your former manner of life and is corrupt through deceitful desires, and to be renewed in the spirit of your minds, and to *put on the new self, created after the likeness of God in true righteousness and holiness.* (Ephesians 4:22-24)

> Do not lie to one another, seeing that you have put off the old self with its practices and have *put on the new self, which is being renewed in knowledge after the image of its Creator.* (Colossians 3:9-10)

As new creations in Christ, we have been transferred from a world of darkness into a kingdom of light. And we are told to put off our old ways: hurtful habits, rebellious attitudes, and all of the sin that clings so closely. We are then told to put on the *new self*—not in order to become something new, but *because* we are already new creations in Christ.

This is consistent with the way the Scriptures speak about identity as it relates to behavior: "Do you not know that a little leaven leavens out the whole lump? Cleanse out the old leaven that you may be a new lump, *as you are really unleavened*" (1 Corinthians 5:6-7). These Christians in Corinth were instructed to align their behavior with who they really were, with their true identity. There were people in the congregation at Corinth who were caught in deep sexual immorality. If anyone in the church was unwilling to repent and align their ways with Christ, the rest of the congregation were instructed to not associate with that person. This is because that person's identity in Jesus Christ should dictate a new behavior. Paul was saying, in effect, "Repent! *Be* an unleavened lump of bread, as you are *already* an unleavened lump of bread." Likewise, our behavior is dictated by our identity. As new creatures in Christ, we must put away our old manner of life and put on the new self, which reflects who we really are in the Jesus.

It is so wonderful for each of us to have been made new creations in Jesus Christ, with a "new self, created after the likeness of God in true righteousness and holiness." When Scripture speaks of holiness here, it is not talking about becoming stern-faced saints, all solemn and grim religiousness. The word *holiness* actually comes from the same root by which we get our word *wholeness*. God is working to make us whole people. It carries with it the idea of completeness, health, and even salvation. Often a person's life is torn apart when they are in bondage to sin. Their lives are hopeless and bankrupt. Sin can shatter the relationship with family and friends. This is the natural death that sin brings. Every person is broken on the inside because of the fall. But God desires to make us whole in Christ—wholly righteous, wholly good, complete and consistent throughout our entire being. This is how we were created to be! And it is a beautiful thing. Holiness is a beautiful thing.

My prayer is that you now see that through our unity with Jesus in His resurrection, Christ now lives inside of us. We are now being saved by Christ's indwelling life more and more each day: "For if while we were enemies we were reconciled to God by the death of his Son, much more, now having been reconciled, *shall we be saved by his life*" (Romans 5:10). Are you being transformed by His life in you? My hope for you is that you draw nearer to Him. For now, we must press ever onwards to explore how we are to further appropriate our position in Christ Jesus.

THE NEW COVENANT

"Behold, the days are coming, declares the Lord,
when I will make a new covenant with the house
of Israel and the house of Judah..."
(Jeremiah 31:31)

THE NATURE OF COVENANTS

Throughout the Scriptures the Lord is revealing His divine character to His people. He declares Himself to be faithful, holy, righteous, just, and good. God cares for the poor and oppressed, and promises to avenge the innocent. And one of God's main attributes is that He is relational. Not only did God create mankind from the dust of the earth, He desires to be in relationship with them. Often when God relates to people He does so by entering into *covenants* with them. For example, God made a covenant with Abraham to prove His faithfulness to His promises (Genesis 15:7-21).

A covenant is a binding agreement that holds two

parties to clearly defined roles and obligations. This was according to the customs of the ancient culture. Covenants were made between individuals, and peoples, and tribes, and nations. God used covenants in order to reveal His divine purposes and to clearly set forth His conditions and promises towards His people.

This is how a covenant would be made: The two parties would take an animal, like a calf or a goat, and would cut it in half from head to tail. The two pieces of the sacrificed animal were laid face up, side by side. The blood of the animal was then allowed to flow towards the center of the two pieces, soaking the ground between them. The parties would then walk through the blood, symbolizing that *if they break their covenant, they would share the same fate as the sacrificed animal they had cut into pieces.* For example, God declared, "And the men who transgressed my covenant and did not keep the terms of the covenant that they made before me, I will make them like the calf that they cut in two and passed between its parts" (Jeremiah 34:18). Thus the blood of the covenant acted as a guarantee, that all the covenant promises would be fulfilled, for if anyone broke their covenant the blood would be upon their head.

Covenants are similar to contracts of this present day, but the obligations are binding and carry much more weight. Frequently today contracts are written but are never kept. Covenants are not so. When two parties enter into a covenant with one another, the agreed upon roles and obligations *must* be met. And when we read about covenants in Scripture, we should think about them in this sense, they are not contracts that can simply be discarded. Covenants are a matter of life and death.

THE OLD COVENANT

After the nation of Israel had been redeemed from slavery in Egypt, they traveled across the Red Sea and through the desert, to Mt. Sinai. It was here that the Lord met them and cut a covenant with His people:

> There Israel encamped before the mountain, while Moses went up to God. The Lord called to him out of the mountain, saying, "Thus you shall say to the house of Jacob, and tell the people of Israel: You yourselves have seen what I did to the Egyptians, and how I bore you on eagle's wings and brought you to myself. Now therefore, if you will indeed obey my voice and keep my covenant, you shall be my treasured possession among all people, for all the earth is mine; and you shall be to me a kingdom of priests and a holy nation. These are the words you shall speak to the people of Israel." So Moses came and called the elders of the people and set before them all these words that the Lord had commanded him. All the people answered together and said, "All that the Lord has spoken we will do." (Exodus 19:2-8)

The words "if you indeed obey my voice and keep my covenant" show that the main condition of this covenant was *obedience*. If Israel kept God's commandments, they would be God's treasured possession among all the nations, a kingdom of priests and a holy nation. Obedience would bring blessing, while disobedience would bring a curse of judgment and destruction (Deuteronomy 11:26-28). The people hastily agreed to the terms of the covenant, understanding that God would be faithful and fulfill His promises in return.

After Israel agreed to the Lord's proposal, Moses climbed to the top of Mt. Sinai in order to meet with God and receive the law. The rocks trembled as they were consumed by a thick cloud in which God descended upon it in devouring fire. It was on top of this frightened mountain that Moses met with the Almighty. God dictated the Ten Commandments to Moses, along with certain civil and ceremonial laws, who then returned to the people to explain all that he was instructed. Moses then confirmed the covenant according to the ancient traditions:

> Then he took the Book of the Covenant and read it in the hearing of the people. And they said, "All that the Lord has spoken we will do, and we will be obedient." And Moses took the blood and threw if on the people and said, "Behold the blood of the covenant that the Lord has made with you in accordance with all these words." (Exodus 24:7-8)

Moses wrote the words that the Lord had spoken on a

scroll called the Book of the Covenant. Israel agreed to obey everything written, so Moses dipped the scroll in blood and threw the blood on the people. This action was symbolic, as if Israel was declaring, "May what happened to this sacrificed animal happen to us if we break our covenant with the Lord!" Thus Israel's covenant with God was confirmed. They agreed, and kept on agreeing, to keep God's commandments. After the covenant was confirmed, God again summoned Moses to meet Him at the top of Sinai. This was in order to give Moses the Ten Commandments carved on tablets of stone:

> The Lord said to Moses, "Come up to ne on the mountain and wait there, that I may give you the tablets of stone, with the law and the commandment, which I have written for their instruction." (Exodus 24:12)

Moses spent forty days and forty nights with the Lord on top of Mt. Sinai. It was at this time that He also received strict instructions about the construction of the tabernacle and the Ark of the Covenant. During these forty days we learn something revealing about the fickle hearts of God's people. *Israel was never faithful to her covenant with the Lord.* Even after freedom from slavery in Egypt, God parting the Red Sea, and feeding them manna from heaven, even after swearing their faithfulness in a covenant of blood, Israel went astray. As quickly as they had promised obedience, they turned aside from the way God instructed them. They were truly a stiff-necked people! Moses had not even returned with the tablets of stone before they had *already* broken every single commandment. And when Moses returned and saw how deep Israel's sin was, his "anger burned hot" (Exodus 32:19). The people had exchanged the truth of God for a lie and formed a golden calf to worship. And in a cryptic gesture, Moses smashed the tablets of stone at the foot of the mountain. After destroying the idol, Moses stood in the gate of the camp:

> Then Moses stood in the gate of the camp and said, "Who is on the Lord's side? Come to me." And all the sons of Levi gathered around him. And he said to them, "This says the Lord God of Israel, 'Put your sword on your side each of you, and go to fro from gate to gate throughout the camp, and each of you kill his brother and his companion and his neighbor.'" And the sons of Levi did according to the word of Moses. And that day about three thousand men of the people fell. (Exodus 32:26-28)

The commandment that promised life brought only death, for three thousand people were slaughtered that day. This covenant with Israel began in failure.

Israel's unfaithfulness at Sinai started a pattern of that remained throughout the entire Old Testament. Remember, *obedience* was the main condition of the covenant. Yet the Israelites never fulfilled their half of the covenant, no matter how the Lord pleaded with them.

Under the leadership of Joshua Israel experienced a brief time of victory as they took possession of the promise land (although even this was mixed with unfaithfulness and failure!). However, after the conquest of the promise land the people quickly went astray again. In their unfaithfulness God gave them over to their enemies, to be plundered by foreign invaders. Yet the Lord was merciful even in times of rebellion, and raised up judges to deliver His people:

> Then the Lord raised up judges, who saved them out of the hand of those who plundered them. Yet they did not listen to their judges, for they whored after other gods and bowed down to them... Whenever the Lord raised up judges for them, the Lord was with the judge, and he saved them from the hand of their enemies all the days of the judge... But whenever the judge died, they turned back and were more corrupt than their fathers... (Judges 2:16-19)

Each new generation became more wicked than the one before it. The writer of Judges gives us a sobering analysis of what the entire 400 year span was like, a refrain that is repeated six times total in the book:

> In those days there was no king in Israel.
> Everyone did what was right in his own eyes. (Judges 21:25)

During the days of the judges everyone did whatever was right in their own eyes. Israel never kept her covenant with the Lord, not for a single day. At the end of this period in Israel's history the prophet Samuel became judge over Israel. And when he was old, he appointed his two sons as judges. However, his sons were dishonorable men and the people did not want them as judges. The elders of Israel came together and demanded that a king be appointed over the nation. This was a tragedy as well, for in demanding a human king they were rejecting *God* as their king. And the Lord in His sovereign wisdom granted the people what they desired:

> And the Lord said to Samuel, "Obey the voice of the people in all that they say to you, for they have not rejected you, but they have rejected me from being king over them. According to the deeds that they have done, from the day I brought them out of Egypt, forsaking me and serving other gods, so they are also doing to you." (1 Samuel 8:7-8)

So began a long line of kings in Israel. Some of the kings were good, some were bad, and many fell somewhere in between. After the reign of King Solomon the nation divided into a northern and southern kingdom. During these days God sent prophets to warn of His judgment and call Israel to repentance. However, because of their unfaithfulness to the Lord the people were eventually led into captivity. But the vital question we must ask is this: Did any of it really help? Did Israel ever fulfill her covenant promises? The answer, of course, is no. The nation of Israel never honored God nor kept His commandments. They were unfaithful to the covenant they had sworn in blood to keep—every day, of every month, of every year.

THE NEW COVENANT

The covenant that the Lord made with Israel at Sinai, which the Scriptures refer to as the Old Covenant, was only part of God's divine plan of redemption. It had its purposes, which later we shall explore. Yet in view of Israel's unfaithfulness to fulfill her covenant, God spoke through the prophet Jeremiah of a *new* covenant:

> "Behold, the days are coming, declares the Lord, when I will make a new covenant with the house of Israel and the house of Judah, not like the covenant that I made with their fathers on the day when I took them by the hand to bring them out of the land of Egypt, my covenant that they broke, thought I was their husband, declares the Lord. But this is the covenant that I will make with the house of Israel after those days, declares the Lord: I will put my law within them, and I will write it on their hearts. And I will be their God, and they shall be my people. And no longer shall each one teach his neighbor and each his brother, saying, 'Know the Lord,' for they shall all know me, from the least of them to the

> greatest, declares the Lord. For I will
> forgive their iniquity, and I will remember
> their sin no more." (Jeremiah 31:31-34)

The Lord declared that the New Covenant was going to be "not like the covenant that I made with their fathers… My covenant that they broke, *though I was their husband*" (Jeremiah 31:32). In saying, "though I was their husband," we understand that the Old Covenant was *really* a covenant of marriage. The Lord betrothed Himself to Israel at Sinai. By accepting His covenant Israel consented to the marriage proposal from God and said, "I do." God had set His heart upon Israel and chose her to be His bride, His treasured possession among all nations. This fact is quite revealing because of what it means. *The Old Covenant was not legalism.* Often the Old Covenant law is assumed to be legalistic, because obedience is the main condition of the covenant. Yet God did not want a legalistic, mechanical relationship with His people, but instead desired something far more valuable—He desired their hearts.

God's love for Israel was boundless, and He longed for her love in return. In the writings of the Old Testament prophets we see Him pleading as a husband for an unfaithful wife (Hosea 2:16-20, Ezekiel 16:30-31). Jesus explained that the greatest commandment, the crux of the whole law, was to "love the Lord your God with all your heart and with all your soul and with all your mind" (Matthew 22:37). This love would manifest itself in holiness and obedience to the Lord. Even today, there are a number of people who are very sincere, desiring to love God and keep His commandments, yet are living under the Old Covenant. They rely on their own best efforts to recommend themselves to God. This is a tragic mistake. Even in their sincerity, their righteous deeds are as filthy rags before God (Isaiah 64:6), because they never can fulfill the Old Covenant requirement of *complete* obedience (Exodus 24:3). And yet they still try. The Old Covenant, then, appears to be the default mode for many Christians. And they will persist in living according to the Old Covenant, unless shown otherwise.

Why didn't the Old Covenant ever work? Why wasn't Israel able to love the Lord and keep His commandments? The answer is this: Israel had a heart of stone, unable to love God (Ezekiel 36:26). The book of Hebrews explains the Old Covenant, declaring, "For he finds fault with them [the people]" (Hebrews 8:8). God didn't find fault with the covenant itself, but *with the people*. Israel would go astray as a wayward wife and follow after false idols. Their hearts were stone, and they worshipped idols made of stone. We are no different. We too are people with stony hearts that hang heavy inside our chests. And no matter how sincere we try to be in our faith, or how much love and devotion towards God we try to conjure, there is nothing *we* can do to change ourselves.

Even though God had promised a New Covenant with His people, He could not simply do away the Old Covenant. Covenants were made to be kept. God had betrothed Himself to Israel, and He must remain faithful to His promises or else He would be shown to be unfaithful as well. So the question is this: What is God to do with unfaithful Israel? What does a husband do when he loves his wife, but she doesn't love him in return?

This brings us to the beauty of the New Covenant.

In the New Covenant, God became a man in Jesus. And Jesus—who was truly God and truly man—did what no man had done before. Jesus, the man, loved God *perfectly*, and He gave God His whole heart. Therefore Jesus took the place of His people and acted as their representative. While the Lord deemed Israel to be a bunch of wild grapes (Isaiah 5:1-7), Jesus declared Himself to be the only True Vine who produces good fruit for God (John 15:1-4). As Israel's representative, Jesus loved God and fulfilled *all* the righteous requirements of the law.

The Savior said of His work, "Do not think that I have come to abolish the Law or the Prophets; I have not come to abolish them but to fulfill them" (Matthew 5:17). When their hearts were not able, Jesus Christ did on Israel's behalf what they could not do themselves. Thus, in Christ, all the stipulations of the Old Covenant were fulfilled! Even more than that—in Jesus all the promises of the New Covenant are fulfilled as well. And this covenant is not just for Israel, but for all who respond to the gospel by faith in Jesus Christ.

THE BLOOD OF THE COVENANT

On the night Jesus was betrayed, He took a cup of wine and declared to His disciples, "Drink of it, all of you, for this is my blood of the new covenant, which is poured out for many for the forgiveness of sins" (Matthew 26:27-28). These words echo what Moses told the Israelites when the Old Covenant was confirmed, "Behold the blood of the covenant that the Lord has made with you in accordance with all these words" (Exodus 24:8). The Old

Covenant was inaugurated with the blood of calves and goats, which Moses sprinkled on the people and the objects used in worship, thus setting them apart for a holy purpose (Hebrews 9:18-21). The New Covenant was inaugurated by the blood of Jesus Christ. His blood was a *guarantee* that God would fulfill all His covenant promises. If one has doubts about the fulfillment of New Covenant promises, they should look to none other than the blood of Jesus. Thus Christ's blood is the blood of the New Covenant, and fulfilled an important promise of the New Covenant: "For I will forgive their iniquity, and I will remember their sin no more" (Jeremiah 31:34).

The contrast between the blood of each covenant is profound, and the New Covenant that Jesus mediates is "better, since it is enacted on *better* promises." (Hebrews 8:6). The flaw of the Old Covenant was that it could never do away with sins. It could never perfect anyone nor give them a righteous standing before God:

> For since the law has but a shadow of the good things to come instead of the true form of these realities, it can never, by the same sacrifices that are continually offered every year, make perfect those who draw near. Otherwise, would they not have ceased to be offered, since the worshipers, having once been cleansed, would no longer have any consciousness of sin? But in these sacrifices there is a reminder of sin every year. *For it is impossible for the blood of bulls and goats to take away sins.* (Hebrews 10:1-4)

The law was only a shadow of things to come, not the reality. The Levitical priesthood could only provide the people with a partial *covering* of their sins, but could never secure their removal. "For it is *impossible* for the blood of bulls and goats to take away sins" (Hebrews 10:4). Day after day, the people had to keep offering the same animal sacrifices. They held yearly festivals as well, such as the Passover, where the priests would sacrifice animals for the sins of the people. *But these animal sacrifices could never take the sins away from the people.* The unending ceremonial sacrifices were a foreboding reminder that their sins still remained.

The difference between the two covenants, then, is the difference between the blood of animals and the blood of Jesus Christ. These blood sacrifices were a shadow of the things to come. Jesus is the reality. John the Baptist declared of Christ, "Behold, the Lamb of God, who *takes away* the sin of the world!" (John 1:29). A lamb cannot take away sins, only God's Lamb can take away sins. Christ is therefore the mediator of a better covenant:

> Therefore he is the mediator of a new covenant, so that those who are called may receive the promised eternal inheritance, since a death has occurred that redeems them from the transgressions committed under the first covenant. For where a will is involved, the death of the one who made it must be established. For a will takes effect only at death, since it is not in force as long as

the one who made it is alive. (Hebrews 9:15-17)

Christ shed His blood to redeem those sins committed under the Old Covenant law. Not only that, the New Covenant was brought into effect at the death of Jesus, "for a will takes effect only at death" (Hebrews 9:17). His blood is surely the blood of the New Covenant. The New Covenant is Jesus' last will and testament, as He is both the will-maker of the covenant, and its executor.

One final point about the finality of the blood of Christ should be made, that we can rest in what He has accomplished. Hebrews speaks of the Levitical priests:

> And every priest stands daily at his service, offering repeatedly the same sacrifices, which can never take away sins. But when Christ had offered for all time a single sacrifice for sins, he sat down at the right hand of God, waiting for that time until his enemies should be made a footstool for His feet. For by a single offering he has perfected for all time those who are being sanctified. (Hebrews 10:11-15)

There were no chairs within the ancient tabernacle, for it was forbidden for the priests to sit down while they offered their services. This is symbolic, that the priests' work was *never* finished. Every day they stood at their services, always offering the same sacrifices, "which can never take away sins" (Hebrews 10:11). This is not so with

Christ. "But when Christ had offered for all time a single sacrifice for sins, he sat down at the right hand of God" (Hebrews 10:12). What did Christ do after His sacrifice? *He sat down.* Why? *His work was finished.* Jesus cried out on the cross, "It is finished!" (John 19:30). For by His one sacrifice—His mighty death on the cross—He has perfected "for all time those who are being sanctified" (Hebrews 10:14). This is the most wonderful news indeed. Jesus was truly "the Lamb of God, who *takes away* the sin of the world!" (John 1:29)

HEARTS TO LOVE GOD AND HIS LAW

The Lord found fault with Israel under the Law of Moses because they were never able to be faithful to their covenant promises. Though they swore faithfulness, they quickly turned astray. They had hearts of stone and were not able to love God or keep His commandments. God had betrothed Himself to His people at Sinai, yet Israel was an unfaithful bride. Her cold heart always strayed, allowing immorality and false idols.

The Lord commanded the prophet Hosea to marry a harlot to illustrate to Israel their spiritual unfaithfulness. While the northern kingdom was enjoying a time of material wealth and prosperity, Hosea warned them of impending destruction and exile at the hands of their enemies. This was God's judgment for breaking their covenant promises with Him (Deuteronomy 28:15-68). Hosea proclaimed a message of sin and judgment to the Lord's unfaithful bride. And yet God also promised a time of future restoration and faithfulness:

"And in that day, declares the Lord, you
will call me 'My Husband,' and no longer
will you call me, 'My Baal.' For I will
remove the names of the Baals from her
mouth, and they shall be remembered by
name no more... And I will betroth you
to me forever. I will betroth you to me in
righteousness and in justice, in steadfast
love and in mercy. I will betroth you to
me in faithfulness. And you shall know
the Lord." (Hosea 2:16-17, 19-20)

Although we are not physical Israel and did not
covenant with the Lord at Sinai, we are no better than
Israel in our ability to love God and keep His
commandments. We all in our hearts have gone astray and
have denied our Creator. The Scriptures teach:

For the wrath of God is revealed from
heaven against all ungodliness and
unrighteousness of men, who by their
unrighteousness suppress the truth. For
what can be known about God is plain to
them, because God has shown it to them.
For his invisible attributes, namely, his
eternal power and divine nature, have
been clearly perceived, ever since the
creation of the world, in the things that
have been made. So they are without
excuse. (Romans 1:18-20)

While the truth about God is evident, humanity suppresses

this truth in unrighteousness. "The heart is deceitful above all things, and desperately sick; who can understand it?" (Jeremiah 17:9). Men have hearts of stone as well, and do not love or honor God as they ought.

One of the great New Covenant promises is that we are given new hearts with God's law written upon them: "I will put my law within them, and I will write it on their hearts" (Jeremiah 31:33). As new creations in Christ, God has performed a heart transplant in us: "I will give you a new heart, and a new spirit I will put within you. And I will remove the heart of stone from your flesh and give you a heart of flesh" (Ezekiel 36:26). In Jesus Christ we have hearts that can begin to love God and delight in His law. This is God's covenant promise to us. Consequently, the Bible teaches that the New Covenant is "written not with ink but with the Spirit of the living God, not on tablets of stone but on tablets of human hearts" (2 Corinthians 3:3). As Christians, we have hearts with His law written upon them that exist only to love and obey God.

While the Old Covenant law promised life, it *really* was a "ministry of death" (Deuteronomy 4:1, 2 Corinthians 3:7). The people had hearts of stone, following a law that was carved in stone. *These are dead things.* The New Covenant, however, has people with hearts of flesh that have God's law written on them by the Spirit of God. Thus the New Covenant is a "ministry of the Spirit," which gives life (2 Corinthians 3:8). When the Israelites broke their covenant with God at Sinai, three thousand people were slaughtered (Exodus 32:26-28). When the apostle Peter stood and preached at Pentecost, three thousand people believed in Jesus, thus crossing from death to life (Acts 2:41). The Old Covenant kills, the New Covenant gives life.

While we will never be perfect in this world, I am thankful that our Redeemer not only changes what we *should* do, but also is changing what we *want* to do. Jesus spoke, "Whoever has my commandments and keeps them, he it is who loves me. And he who loves me will be loves by my Father, and I will love him and manifest myself to him" (John 14:21). Do you love Jesus? "And by this we know that we have come to know him, if we keep his commandments. Whoever says 'I know him' but does not keep his commandments is a liar, and the truth is not in him" (1 John 2:3-4). May the Holy Spirit teach us to love God and to keep His commandments as we ought.

KNOWING GOD

The Lord declared yet another New Covenant promise, proclaiming, "No longer shall each one teach his neighbor and each his brother, saying, 'Know the Lord,' for they shall all know me, from the least of them to the greatest, declares the Lord" (Jeremiah 31:34). It is a promise of relationship and intimate fellowship with God. Throughout history we see that one of God's deepest desires is to dwell with man. In Genesis the Lord would walk through the Garden of Eden in the cool of the day (Genesis 3:8). I get the impression from the text that this was not unusual, but that the Lord would regularly walk about the garden to fellowship with His people. However, when Adam and Eve sinned God could no longer dwell with his sinful creatures. The story of redemption is then a giant rescue mission, where God is working to bring mankind *back* into paradise so that we may dwell with Him.

In the Old Testament God was able to dwell with Israel in the tabernacle. The tabernacle allowed God to be in the midst of His covenant people, but also acted as a barrier, that in His holiness God would not destroy the entire encampment of Israel. God spoke to Moses, "Say to the people of Israel, 'You are a stiff-necked people; if for a single moment I should go up among you, I would consume you'" (Exodus 33:5). If the Holy God were to be amongst His sinful people for even a single *instant* He would destroy them. The tabernacle was the solution to this. However, as in the rest of the Old Covenant, this dwelling was on the condition of obedience: "If you walk in my statutes and observe my commandments and do them... I will make my dwelling among you, and my soul shall not abhor you. And I will walk among you and will be your God, and you shall be my people" (Leviticus 26:3, 11-12).

The temple that Solomon built was the legitimate successor to the tabernacle. King Solomon declared it "a place for [God] to dwell forever" (1 Kings 8:13). The temple was supposed to provide a permanent dwelling place for the presence of the Lord. Yet even then no one could know God while He remained in the Holy of Holies. The temple was eventually destroyed by foreign invaders. Even the earthly temple could not provide a permanent dwelling place for the Lord. Would God's desire to dwell with humanity be left unsatisfied?

In Christ's incarnation God did something radical: He clothed Himself in flesh and bone and dwelt among

His people: "And the Word became flesh and *dwelt* among us" (John 1:14). The earthly temple that Solomon built only whispered of the glory of Christ, for Christ was the temple of God while He walked this earth. Jesus declared to the Jews in Jerusalem, "'Destroy this temple, and in three days I will raise it up...' He was speaking about the temple of his body" (John 2:19, 21).

However, God had an even more glorious goal in humanity's redemption. This is the fulfillment of His New Covenant promise that we will know Him (Jeremiah 31:34). The Most High no longer dwells in buildings made by human hands, but instead He has made His temple inside of each of us:

> For we are the temple of the living God; as God said, "I will make my dwelling among them and walk among them, and I will be their God, and they shall be my people." (2 Corinthians 6:16)

We are the temple of the Holy Spirit. Now we can know the Lord through the indwelling of His Spirit: "And I will put my Spirit within you..." (Ezekiel 36:27). The Holy Spirit mediates Christ's presence to us, drawing us to trust Jesus to be our all in all.

The fulfillment of this New Covenant promise was on the basis of Christ's glorification. All of God's promises are fulfilled are on the basis of Jesus Christ and His work. This is how we can have confidence that the Spirit has been poured out onto the body of Christ. Peter stood and preached at Pentecost:

"This Jesus God raised up, and of that we are all witnesses. *Being therefore exalted at the right hand of God, and having received from the Father the promise of the Holy Spirit*, he has poured out this that you yourselves are seeing and hearing... Let all the house of Israel therefore know for certain that God has made him both Lord and Christ, this Jesus who you crucified." (Acts 2:32-33, 36)

It is on the basis of Christ's glorification that the Holy Spirit has been given. Jesus cried out at the Feast of Tabernacles,

On the last day of the feast, the great day, Jesus stood up and cried out, "If anyone thirsts, let him come to me and drink. Whoever believes in me, as the Scripture has said, 'Out of his heart will flow rivers of living water.'" Now this he said about the Spirit, whom those who believed in him were to receive, for as yet *the Spirit had not been given, because Jesus was not yet glorified.* (John 7:37-39)

The reason we've been gifted the Holy Spirit is *not* to show our own greatness, but instead to prove how great is Jesus Christ. The Son has been glorified and is exalted at the right hand of the Father. By His work our bodies have been made into the very temple of God.

Do you thirst? You may come to Christ and drink

freely. His Spirit lives inside of you and wants to draw you closer to Jesus. God desires you to reach out to Him and find Him and know Him.

Knowing God is a New Covenant promise that is being fulfilled, and the fullness of this promise will not be realized until eternity. The Holy Spirit is "the guarantee of our inheritance until we acquire possession of it" (Ephesians 1:14). He is the Lord's down payment. God's ultimate dwelling place with us will be in heaven: "And I heard a loud voice from the throne saying, "Behold, the dwelling place of God is with man. He will dwell with them, and they will be his people, and God Himself will be with them as their God"" (Revelation 21:3). *No longer must God dwell in a temple, for He will be with His people, and we shall know Him.* John described the New Jerusalem, "And I saw no temple in the city, for its temple is the Lord God the Almighty and the Lamb" (Revelation 21:22). And yet as we wait for eternity, we can know God *today*, through the indwelling of His Holy Spirit. Do you desire to know God? Jesus Christ has prepared the way. Seek His face today and you can begin to know the Lord in a real and vibrant way.

WALKING IN GOD'S STATUTES

What about the final promise of the New Covenant? God has placed His Spirit within us and has promised to cause us to keep His commandments: "I will put my Spirit within you, and cause you to walk in my statutes and be careful to obey my rules" (Ezekiel 36:27). This boldly promises to do something that has never been done before—keep the very commandments that Israel failed to obey. How is such a life of obedience possible?

Here, then, is the wonder of all wonders, the wonder of the ages, the very light of things hoped for: Jesus is ready *again* to love God and keep His commandments. Jesus Christ desires to live His life through *us*, if we would only look to Him to do so. In the same way that Jesus fulfilled the Law of Moses on Israel's behalf, Christ will be the fulfillment of the law in us. The apostle Paul explains the New Covenant:

> Such is the confidence that we have through Christ toward God. Not that we are sufficient in ourselves to claim anything as coming from us, but *our sufficiency is from God*, who has made us competent to be ministers of a new covenant, not of the letter but of the Spirit. For the letter kills, but the Spirit gives life (2 Corinthians 3:4-6)

In the New Covenant we do not place any confidence in ourselves, in our own righteousness or abilities, but instead look to Jesus Christ to be our sufficiency in all things. Jesus will give us obedience. The presence of His indwelling life will cause us to begin to delight in and keep God's law.

The prophet Isaiah ascribes to Jesus: "I will give you as a covenant for the people" (Isaiah 42:6). Christ *Himself* is a covenant, for all of the blessings of the New Covenant are accomplished in Jesus and His work. Even more than that, Jesus is the *guarantee* and *guarantor* of the New

Covenant (Hebrews 7:22). Not only is the blood of Christ God's guarantee that all the covenant promises *will* be fulfilled, Jesus is also the *guarantor*—the sole instrument through which all the New Covenant promises are achieved. It is His death, His resurrection, His glorification, and His active obedience through which all the covenant promises are fulfilled. We only trust in Jesus Christ by faith. Thus the successfulness of the New Covenant is based upon Christ's faithfulness to fulfill *both* ends of the covenant. We must turn from trusting in dead works and instead look to Jesus Christ to be our sufficiency in all things. Jesus taught His disciples, "I am the vine; you are the branches. Whoever abides in me and I in him, he it is that bears much fruit, for apart from me you can do *nothing*" (John 15:5). We must feel the weight of His words. We must keep God's commandments, and yet we cannot keep them apart from Christ's obedience in us. While we will never be perfect in this age, Christ *will* begin fulfilling the law in us, if we would only look to Him in faith.

ENTERING INTO THE NEW COVENANT

How are we to enter into this covenant with God? *It is by faith in Christ.* The gospel is this: "That Christ died for our sins in accordance with the Scriptures, that he was buried, that he was raised on the third day in accordance with the Scriptures" (1 Corinthians 15:3-4). When we believe in the resurrection of Christ and confess with our mouth that Jesus is Lord, we are saved (Romans 10:9). Christ's blood in the blood of the covenant (Matthew

26:27-28). Just as when Moses threw the blood onto the people of Israel at Sinai, when we have been covered by the blood of Jesus, we have entered into this covenant with God. This comes by faith alone in Jesus Christ. And just as we respond to the gospel by faith, we live by faith in Jesus:

> For I am not ashamed of the gospel, for it is the power of God for salvation to everyone who believes, to the Jew first and also to the Greek. For in it the righteousness of God is revealed from faith for faith, as it is written, *"The righteousness shall live by faith."* (Romans 1:16-17)

The promises of the New Covenant are applied by faith in Jesus Christ. We must learn to continually lean our whole weight upon Jesus—every day, of every month, of every year.

Do you see the promises of the New Covenant being fulfilled in your life? God is required to fulfill both ends of this covenant. The more the Spirit teaches us to look to Christ, the more His promises will be fulfilled in us. However, at any time we can choose to take our eyes off of Jesus and live according to the Old Covenant again. In the Old Covenant we struggle in our own strength for an obedience we cannot ever produce. This will only bring death. No, let us lay aside every hindrance, "looking to Jesus, the founder and perfecter of our faith" (Hebrews 12:2). Jesus will be faithful to fulfill His covenant with us.

CHAPTER 06 – THE LAW AND THE GOSPEL

Likewise, my brothers, you also have died to the
law through the body of Christ. (Romans 7:4)

HOW THEN SHOULD WE LIVE?

"The law was given through Moses; grace and truth came through Jesus Christ" (John 1:17). We have covered some tremendous truth so far, truth in Christ that God can use to transform lives. In Christ we are completely righteous and acceptable to God. Our unity with Jesus in His death has freed us from slavery to the power of sin. Likewise, our unity with Christ in His resurrection has given us a second birth. Now the very life of Jesus Christ indwells each believer. Finally, we explored how Jesus fulfilled all the stipulations of the Old Covenant, and He is the guarantor of the New Covenant, which is enacted upon better promises.

Many Christians have opened the Scriptures to discover all the truths we have been exploring, but still fall short of the spiritual reality and freedom Christ offers. For example, they may read in Romans that through the death of Jesus they have been set free from sin (Romans 6:6-7), but still remain defeated and in bondage to the power of sin. Likewise, another may learn of the New Covenant promise of a new heart with God's law written on it, and that the Spirit will cause them to walk in His statutes, but in their experience they do not see this promise being fulfilled. Many Christians live lives plagued with drudgery and emptiness. Why is this? I myself have experienced entire seasons in my life of moral failures, depression, spiritual apathy, even boredom. I've wrestled with this question: *Why do we so often fail?*

I am convinced that reason so many stumble is because they do not know their proper relationship to the law of God. While those in Jesus Christ have a new relationship to the law, many Christians still use the law as a means by which they can recommend themselves to God. For example, there are many believers who want a bunch of rules and instructions that they can follow to know that they are righteous and grow in the Lord. This is a grave mistake. As we shall see, placing ourselves under *any* law as a means of righteousness only leads to bondage and failure. The Christian's proper relationship to the law is described in Romans:

> For sin will have no dominion over you,
> since you are not under law but under
> grace. (Romans 6:14)

Here we find that we can experience a practical deliverance from sin. How? *Because we no longer live under the law, but live by grace*. Grace is God's divine favor towards us. It is Him giving us what we do *not* deserve, namely, the finished work of Christ. As we explore this topic, we shall see that it is not enough just to know that we have been set free from sin, but we must also understand that we have been released from the law, from the burden of serving God by means of the old written code. "The law was given through Moses; grace and truth came through Jesus Christ" (John 1:17).

GRACE AND WORKS

During the first century the church in Galatia was in trouble. Their congregation had been infiltrated by Judiazers—who taught that those whom came to Christ must *also* obey the Law of Moses as a means of righteousness. They were mixing grace with works, the gospel of Jesus Christ with the law. This was a serious heresy, one that places people in bondage, and if followed could even keep people from salvation (Galatians 5:2-4). Sadly, there are forms of this teaching rampant in the church today, whenever someone mixes law with the gospel. The apostle Paul writes to the Galatians:

> Tell me, you who desire to be under the law, do you not listen to the law? For it is written that Abraham had two sons, one by a slave woman and one by a free woman. But the son of the slave was born according to the flesh, while the son of the free woman was born through

> promise. Now this may be interpreted allegorically; these women are two covenants. One is from Mount Sinai, bearing children for slavery; she is Hagar. (Galatians 4:21-24)

Abraham had two sons. One was born according to the flesh with a slave woman, and the other came through God's promise. These two children represent two covenants. What must have been scandalous to the early Jewish Christians, however, was what covenant each child represented. One covenant came from Mount Sinai, the other from Jerusalem. The covenant from Mount Sinai gives birth to bondage, and its mother is Hagar (Galatians 4:24). This would have been an offense to the Jew! They would have felt that the apostle Paul had his facts backwards, for it was at Sinai that God gave them the law and made them a free people. The Jews would have insisted that they were children of Sarah, the free woman, able to inherit the promises God made to Abraham. But this is not so. Hagar's child, born according to the flesh, represents the Old Covenant and the law.

In the covenant of law the children of Israel gathered at Mount Sinai and heard the commandments. They proclaimed with one voice, "All the words that the Lord has spoken we will do" (Exodus 24:3). And Moses splashed the blood on the people, for if they broke this covenant their own blood would be upon them. And we already know what happened—they *never* kept their covenant. The Law of Moses was never fulfilled and brought them only death and condemnation. *And this is why the law is bondage and is associated with Hagar.* And we shall explore later the purpose of the law, and how it is slavery if we use it as a means of righteousness.

The New Covenant is represented by Abraham's son, Isaac, and came by promise (Galatians 4:28). This son was born by the free woman, Sarah. In fact, if we search the Scriptures we shall find that the gospel always comes by promise and is never a condition of human works or effort. At Sinai the Lord did not make *any* promises. Israel made all the promises. Yet in the New Covenant God makes all the promises which He faithfully fulfills. Beginning in the Garden of Eden the Lord promised the Messiah:

> "I will put enmity between you and the woman, and between your offspring and her offspring; he shall bruise your head, and you shall bruise his heel" (Genesis 3:15)

Jesus Christ would be the promised offspring of the woman—the eternal Word of God would become flesh and dwell among His people (John 1:14). His heel would be bruised by the serpent by His death on the cross, but in doing would crush the serpent's head. *This was God's promise to His fallen creatures.* It was not conditional, but based upon God's faithfulness to His promises.

God made other promises. Hundreds of years after Adam, the Lord declared His promises to His servant, Abraham:

> Now the Lord said to Abram, "Go from your country and your kindred and your

father's house to the land that I will show you. And I will make of you a great nation, and I will bless you and make your name great, so that you will be a blessing. I will bless those who bless you, and him who dishonors you I will curse, and in you all the families of the earth will be blessed." (Genesis 12:1-3)

God promised Abraham to give him a land, and to make him a great nation, and that through him all peoples of the earth would be blessed. This blessing through which all peoples would be blessed would be Jesus Christ, who came to the earth to ransom people for God. The Lord confirmed His promises in a covenant. When He made this covenant with Abraham, He commanded him to bring five animals (Genesis 15:9). Abraham cut them in half according to the ancient tradition, and waited for God to meet him.

As the sun was going down, a deep sleep fell on Abram. And behold, dreadful and great darkness fell upon him… When the sun had gone down and it was dark, behold, a smoking fire pot and a flaming torch passed between the pieces. On that day the Lord made a covenant with Abram. (Genesis 15:12, 17-18).

Abraham did not walk through the blood, the Lord Himself passed through the blood! And so God swore His covenant to Abraham. This covenant was *not* based upon Abraham's obedience or works, but was based upon the true promises of God.

Likewise, the Lord made a covenant with King David:

> "When your days are fulfilled and you lie down with your fathers, I will raise up your offspring after you, who shall come from your body, and I will establish his kingdom. He shall build a house for my name, and I will establish the throne of his kingdom forever. I will be to him a father, and he shall be to me a son. Whenever he commits iniquity, I will discipline him with the rod of men, with the stripes of the sons of men, but my steadfast love will not depart from him."
> (2 Samuel 7:12-15)

God promised King David that his offspring would sit on the throne forever. Jesus Christ is the root of David and will sit on the throne as king for all eternity. Jesus was disciplined "with the rod of men, with the stripes of the sons of men" when He was made sin on the cross and died to redeem us to God (2 Corinthians 5:21). Again, this was not a conditional covenant like at Sinai, but came by God's faithful promise to David.

And finally the Lord declared His New Covenant through the prophets:

> "Behold, the days are coming, declares the Lord, when I will make a new

covenant with the house of Israel and the house of Judah, not like the covenant that I made with their fathers on the day when I took them by the hand to bring them out of the land of Egypt, my covenant that they broke, thought I was their husband, declares the Lord. But this is the covenant that I will make with the house of Israel after those days, declares the Lord: I will put my law within them, and I will write it on their hearts. And I will be their God, and they shall be my people. And no longer shall each one teach his neighbor and each his brother, saying, 'Know the Lord,' for they shall all know me, from the least of them to the greatest, declares the Lord. For I will forgive their iniquity, and I will remember their sin no more." (Jeremiah 31:31-34)

This covenant would be not be like the Sinai covenant, which Israel broke. It was not to come by obedience to the law, but by promise. Throughout the Bible the gospel is based upon the promises of God and not human works. The New Covenant was given by promise and to be received by faith alone. In fact, the New Covenant was promised long before the law was given! The apostle Paul writes:

To give a human example, brothers: even with a man-made covenant, no one annuls or adds to it once it has been ratified. Now the promises were made to Abraham and to his offspring. It does not say, "And to offsprings," referring to many, but referring to one, "And to your offspring," who is Christ. This is what I mean: the law, which came 430 years afterwards, does not annul a covenant previously ratified by God, so as to make the promise void. *For if the inheritance comes by the law, it no longer comes by promise; but God gave it to Abraham by a promise.* (Galatians 3:15-18).

When we try to earn the promises of God by works of the law, we get ourselves into trouble. The New Covenant promise of the gospel is to be received by grace through faith and not by works (Ephesians 2:8). *In fact, every spiritual blessing we possess in Christ is to be received by faith alone.* If there is one thing we must *do* to receive the promises of God, we place ourselves back under the law and risk forfeiting the promise. This leads only to legalism and failure. Now, we must ask ourselves: What then is the purpose of God's law in our lives?

THE PURPOSE OF THE LAW

The Old Covenant law was *bondage* and only brought forth children for slavery (Galatians 4:24-25). Does this mean that somehow the law of God was bad? No! The book of Romans raises the same argument: "What shall we say? That the law is sin? By no means!" (Romans 7:7).

Of course the law isn't evil. We shall see that the real problem of the law is with *ourselves*. "For we know that the law is spiritual, but I am of the flesh, sold under sin" (Romans 7:14). Let us look at the mighty purposes of the law.

The law reveals sin. The law declares in objective truths what is right and wrong, and what is pleasing to the Lord. The undeniable words are carved in stone. "Yet if it had not been for the law, I would not have known sin. I would not have known what it is to covet is the law had not said, 'You shall not covet'" (Romans 7:7). Apart from the law we would not know what sin was. In this example, the apostle Paul uses the one commandment that deals exclusively with an *internal* struggle. God's law reveals that sin is more than just outward actions, but is a matter of the heart as well. For example, many people think that because they haven't physically committed adultery, or murder, or any of the other commandments, that they are innocent. They reduce the commandments to an external standard, judging only the physical actions of men. Of course none of the commandments are merely external, as Jesus taught:

> "You have heard that it was said to those of old, 'You shall not murder; and whoever murders will be liable to judgment.' But I say to you that everyone who is angry with his brother will be liable to judgment... You have heard that it was said, 'You shall not commit adultery.' But I say to you that everyone who looks at a woman with lustful intent

had already committed adultery with her in his heart." (Matthew 5:21-22, 27-28)

Paul was a Pharisee, and his desire to keep the commandments consumed him. He had zeal for the Law of Moses. And by all accounts, it appears that he did a good job at keeping the law, at least externally. But after he read the tenth commandment, the commandment that dealt with who he was on the *inside*, he saw what was inside of himself. He knew he was a sinner. The law revealed the wickedness inside of Paul. He was allowed to see inside of his heart, and all kinds of covetousness had been revealed. When Paul read the commandment, "You shall not covet," He knew he was a law breaker and desperately needed forgiveness. This is the first purpose of the law, to reveal sin.

The law provokes sin. The law not only exposes sin, but sin is actually *provoked* by the law. "For while we were living in the flesh, our sinful passions, *aroused by the law*, were at work in our members to bear fruit for death" (Romans 7:5). The apostle Paul revisits his example of coveting: "But sin, seizing an opportunity through the commandment, produced in me all kinds of covetousness. Apart from the law, sin lies dead" (Romans 7:8). How wicked we are! Sin uses the holy law of God to make us sin even more. Our experiences bear witness to this. Personally, when I am told that there is something I am not allowed to do—or worse, something I *must* do—I resist the commandment with every fiber of my being. Sin uses the law to keep me from doing what I ought. This is universal to all of humanity. Sin, seizing an opportunity through the law, breeds in our hearts all kinds of rebellion and evil.

The law condemns sin. The law not only exposes and provokes sin, but it condemns it as well:

> I was once alive apart from the law, but when the commandment came, sin came alive and I died. The very commandment that promised life proved to be death to me. For sin, seizing an opportunity through the commandment, deceived me and through it killed me. (Romans 7:9-11)

When Paul talks about sin coming alive and him dying, he is speaking of the condemnation of the law. He says that there was a time when he was alive apart from the law. But when the law revealed the rampant covetousness in his heart, he felt the full condemnation of the law. The law that promised life to him proved only to be a ministry of death. *And this is why the law is bondage.* It is bondage not because the law itself is bad, but because we are sinful. The law measures that sin and condemns us before a holy God.

The law is ruthless. It never rewards us when we actually obey it, or gives us a hearty congratulation for keeping the commandments. The law was given to expose sin, provoke sin, and condemn sin. From this we can see that the ultimate purpose of the law was to bring us to an end of ourselves. It was never given with the understanding that men would fulfill the law and secure an eternal righteousness before God, but instead to show them how desperately wicked their hearts are, that they might cry out to Him for mercy, forgiveness, and inner healing.

The law was a schoolmaster, then, given to lead men to Jesus Christ for salvation:

> Now before faith came, we were held captive under the law, imprisoned until the coming faith would be revealed. So then, the law was our guardian until Christ came, in order that we might be justified by faith. But now that faith has come, we are no longer under a guardian. (Galatians 3:23-25)

The law was not given as a means of righteousness or justification. "We ourselves are Jews by birth and not Gentile sinners; yet we know that *a person is not justified by works of the law but through faith in Jesus Christ*" (Galatians 2:15-16). It was to Israel that the law was given. Yet even Jewish Christians should understand that men are justified by faith in Jesus Christ, and not by works of the law. The law reveals our wickedness, that we might call out to Him for forgiveness! Jesus challenged the Pharisees, declaring: "Go and learn what this means, 'I desire mercy, not sacrifice.' For I came not to call the righteous, but sinners" (Matthew 9:13).

Now, here is the vital point: We are justified by faith in Christ apart from the law. After becoming Christians, how then do we grow? Justification comes by faith alone in Jesus, what about sanctification? Does sanctification come by works of the law? The answer, of course, is *no*. The same gospel that saves also sanctifies. Tragically, many Christians use the law (or worse, create their own "law") as a means of growth. They are mixing the law and the gospel, works and grace. This was the Galatian heresy:

> O foolish Galatians! Who has bewitched you? It was before your eyes that Jesus Christ was publicly portrayed as crucified. Let me ask you only this: Did you receive the Spirit by works of the law or by hearing with faith? Are you so foolish? Having begun by the Spirit, are you now being perfected by the flesh? Did you suffer so many things in vain—if indeed it was in vain? Does he who supplies the Spirit to you and works miracles among you do so by works of the law, or by hearing with faith—just as Abraham "believed God, and it was counted to him as righteousness"? (Galatians 3:1-6)

Sanctification is a work of God alone, one that comes by faith in Jesus. It does not come by works of the law. But because we were born into a covenant of works in Adam, where we know we must build a perfect righteousness to stand before God, law is what comes natural to us. The Old Covenant, then, is the default setting for our flesh. Our flesh *likes* the law. We foolishly believe we can keep the law, and even after coming to Christ we believe we can be perfected in our flesh by works of the law. This is futile: "Are you so foolish? Having begun by the Spirit, are you now being perfected by the flesh?" (Galatians 3:3). Even if we are well meaning, we cannot achieve the promises of God by works of the law. They must come by faith in Jesus Christ, "whom God made our wisdom and our righteousness and sanctification and redemption" (1 Corinthians 1:30).

If we claim that there is even one thing that we must *do* in order to recommend ourselves to God, or grow in our relationship with Him, we place ourselves back under the *whole* law:

> For all who rely on works of the law are under a curse; for it is written, "Cursed be everyone who does not abide by all things written in the Book of the Law, and do them." Now it is evident that no one is justified before God by the law, for "The righteous shall live by faith." But the law is not of faith, rather "The one who does them shall live by them." Christ redeemed us from the curse of the law by becoming a curse for us—for it is written, "Cursed if everyone who is hanged on a tree"—so that in Christ Jesus the blessing of Abraham might come to the Gentiles, so that we might receive the promised Spirit through faith. (Galatians 3:10-14)

If we accept one law as a means by which we stand before God, or even for means of sanctification, we are under a curse. Yet Christ has redeemed us from the curse of the law. We must cut off all ties to the law as a means of righteousness, and look to Jesus Christ.

DEAD TO THE LAW

In Romans is a powerful illustration of our new relationship to the law in Christ. These are profound spiritual insights into our death with Jesus:

> Or do you not know, brothers—for I am speaking to those who know the law— that the law is binding on a person only as long as he lives? Thus a married woman is bound by law to her husband while he lives, but if her husband dies she is released from the law of marriage. Accordingly, she will be called an adulteress if she lives with another man while her husband is alive. But if her husband dies, she is free from that law, and if she marries another man she is not an adulteress. (Romans 7:1-3)

In this illustration there are three distinct entities: the woman, her husband, and the law of marriage that binds them together. Here we see that the claims of the law remain upon a person until death. "Or do you not know, brothers—for I am speaking to those who know the law— that the law is binding on a person only as long as he lives?" (Romans 7:1). We do not concern ourselves with keeping the law after we have died. In this illustration, we are given the law of marriage. Once someone has died, the law of marriage no longer binds them. However, if a married woman tries to live with another man while her husband is still alive, what does the law say to her? It will call her what she is—an adulteress! "Accordingly, she will be called an adulteress if she lives with another man while her husband is alive" (Romans 7:3). This is important to understand. A woman *cannot* live with another man if she is married to her husband, or else the law will condemn her. Only *death* will bring about the end of her relationship and thus release her from the law of marriage.

And what does the law say to the woman once her husband has died? Can the law then tell her where she can go, or who she can be with or marry? Of course not. Once the woman's husband has died, the law has *nothing* to say to her. "If her husband dies, she is free from that law, and if she marries another man she is not an adulteress" (Romans 7:3). Death has ended the woman's former relationship and has *released* her from the law of marriage. So we see here that a death has changed the woman's relationship to the law. Not only did death release the woman from her husband, it *also* released her from the law. In effect, the death of the first husband has made the woman dead to the law. Now, then, we must understand the application of this illustration:

> Likewise, my brothers, you also have died to the law through the body of Christ, so that you may belong to another, to him who has been raised from the dead, in order that we may bear fruit for God. For while we were living in the flesh, our sinful passions, aroused by the law, were at work in our members to bear fruit for death. But now we are released from the law, having died to that which held us

captive, so that we serve not under the
old written code but in the new life of the
Spirit. (Romans 7:4-6)

In this illustration we see that *we* are the woman. That is
clearly where the apostle places us—"Likewise, my
brothers, you *also* have died to the law through the body of
Christ" (Romans 7:4). And who was our husband? As we
have already seen, our first husband was Adam and the
power of sin that enslaved us in Adam, the old life and
nature which we were born into. We were bound to sin,
by virtue of Adam, and there was no way that we could be
released from that relationship without the law calling us
an adulteress.

How were we released from our union to Adam?
How were we delivered from our first husband? We have
already seen the answer. We were released from our old
life in Adam through our unity with Jesus Christ in His
death. "We know that our old self was crucified with Him
in order that the body of sin might be brought to nothing"
(Romans 6:6).

Jesus Christ came and—as we have already seen—He
became the first husband. On the cross, Jesus was made sin
for us. "For our sake He made Him to be sin who knew
no sin, so that in Him we might become the righteousness
of God" (2 Corinthians 5:21).

Jesus became the first husband, our sinful heritage in
Adam, and when He died we were released from our
union with Adam. But what is important for us to see is
how His death has *also* changed our relationship to the law:
*When Christ was made sin on our behalf and died, we were released
from the law.* "Likewise, my brothers, you also have died to

the law through the body of Christ... We are released from the law, having died to that which held us captive" (Romans 7:4, 6).

This declaration of a change in relationship to the law comes first to the Jew: "Or do you not know, brothers— for I am speaking to those who know the law" (Romans 7:1). Israel had made a covenant with God at Sinai. They were the ones who knew the law. This covenant was binding and had to be fulfilled. Consequently, not only did Jesus Christ fulfill the law, His death fundamentally changed the Jewish Christian's relationship to the law. Likewise, although the Gentiles were without law, they still have law written on their conscience (Romans 2:12-16). So now all are free to delight in Christ.

And why again must we be released from the law? Why is the law bondage? It is because we are unable to bear fruit for God by works of the law. "We know that a person is not justified by works of the law but through faith in Jesus Christ" (Galatians 2:16). We are justified by grace though faith in Christ.

Likewise, our sanctification comes by faith in Christ and not by law. "Let me ask you only this: Did you receive the Spirit by works of the law or by hearing with faith? Are you so foolish? Having begun by the Spirit, are you now being perfected by the flesh?" (Galatians 3:2-3). And this is why we must be released from the law, to bear fruit for God in the new life of the Spirit:

> Likewise, my brothers, you also have died
> to the law through the body of Christ, so
> that we may belong to another, to him
> who has been raised from the dead, in

order that we may bear fruit for God.
(Romans 7:4)

We died to the law for a reason, so that we may belong
to the risen Christ, in order to bear fruit for God. Jesus
Christ is the bridegroom, and we are the bride. He will
bear fruit through His indwelling life in us. Will we cease
doing for God and allow what Christ has *done* to change
us? We must not trust in works of the law but in the
gospel of Jesus Christ. The same gospel that was enough
for our justification is also enough for our sanctification.
Look to Jesus by faith and walk in the new life of the
Spirit, and He will bear good fruit in you. "The law was
given through Moses; grace and truth came through Jesus
Christ" (John 1:17).

CHAPTER 07 – WALKING BY THE SPIRIT

*If we live by the Spirit, let us also walk by the
Spirit. (Galatians 5:25)*

THE NEW COVENANT: A MINISTRY OF THE SPIRIT

In the preceding chapter we alluded to a single verse
in Romans: "Now we are released from the law, having
died to that which held us captive, so that we serve not
under the old written code but in the new life of the Spirit"
(Romans 7:6). Here is a bit of a paradox: Even though we
have been released from serving God by works of the law,
we *still* serve God. How do we do this? Now we serve
God "*in the new life of the Spirit.*"

The apostle Paul describes the New Covenant as a
"ministry of the Spirit" (2 Corinthians 3:8). In this the
Lord fulfills His covenant promise: "And I will put my
Spirit within you, and cause you to walk in my statutes and
be careful to obey my rules" (Ezekiel 36:27). We
understand, then, that we died to the law for a grand

purpose. We died to the law in order that Christ might dwell inside each of us, and Jesus—by the agency of the Holy Spirit—would be the fulfillment of the law in us. This is how we can possess lives of true righteousness and holiness. However, we cannot *simultaneously* serve God according to both the Old and the New Covenant. At any moment we are either serving the Lord by His grace or by works of the law. We are either living by faith in Jesus or foolishly striving to grow by the flesh. The New Covenant is giving us life in Christ or the Old Covenant is killing us. And if we want to see God's New Covenant promises fulfilled in our lives, we must learn how to walk by the Spirit. Remember, we died to the law in order that we may belong to another: Jesus Christ, our risen savior. "Likewise, my brothers, you also have died to the law through the body of Christ, *so that you may belong to another, to him who has been raised from the dead*, in order that we may bear fruit for God" (Romans 7:4). All of this has passed so that we might walk in the new life of the Spirit.

THE HOLY SPIRIT

Ezekiel was a prophet during the Jewish exile to the Assyrian empire. He was one of the prophets through with the Lord promised the New Covenant to a broken people:

> And I will give you a new heart, and a new spirit I will put within you. I will remove the heart of stone from your flesh and give you a heart of flesh. And I will

> put my Spirit within you, and cause you to
> walk in my statutes and be careful to obey
> my rules. (Ezekiel 36:26-27)

It was in the context of *that* promise—the promise that He would one day place His Spirit inside of them—that the Lord then gave Ezekiel this dramatic vision:

> The hand of the Lord was upon me, and
> he brought me out in the Spirit of the
> Lord and set me down in the middle of
> the valley; it was full of bones. And he
> led me around among them, and behold,
> there were very many on the surface of
> the valley, and behold, they were very dry.
> (Ezekiel 37:1-2)

God took Ezekiel to a vast valley that was covered with white-washed bones. These bones had been lying in the sun for a long time and were very dry. After leading His servant around the bones, He challenged Ezekiel with this question:

> And he said to me, "Son of man, can
> these bones live?" And I answered, "O
> Lord God, you know." (Ezekiel 36:3)

Ezekiel did not know the meaning of the vision, whether the bones could live again, but God knew. The Lord is not only Creator, but He is also Redeemer. He not only gives life, He brings life to those who have died. If God wanted these bones to live again, *He* could do it. And so the Lord Almighty again challenged His prophet:

> The he said to me, "Prophesy over these bones, and say to them, O dry bones, hear the word of the Lord. Thus says the Lord God to these bones: Behold, I will cause breath to enter you, and you shall live. And I will lay sinews upon you, and will cause flesh to come upon you, and cover you with skin, and put breath in you, and you shall live, and you shall know that I am the Lord." (Ezekiel 37:4-6)

God commanded Ezekiel to prophecy to the valley of dry bones. He told Ezekiel to declare to the bones that *breath* would enter them, and they would live. He would put *breath* inside these bones, and they would live, and would know that He is the Lord. The trembling prophet did as he was commanded:

> So I prophesied as I was commanded. And as I prophesied, there was a sound, and behold, a rattling, and the bones came together, bone to its bone. And I looked, and behold, there were sinews on them, and flesh had come upon them, and skin had covered them. But there was no breath in them. (Ezekiel 37:7-8)

The surprised bones began to rattle and move! Each bone came together, bone upon bone, and flesh and skin covered the hones. *But there was no breath in them.* The Lord urged the prophet:

> Then he said to me, "Prophesy to the breath; prophesy, son of man, and say to the breath, Thus says the Lord God: Come from the four winds, O breath, and breathe on these slain, that they may live." (Ezekiel 37:9)

Ezekiel would prophesy to the *breath*, and from the four winds of the earth the *breath* would come, and the valley of dry bones would finally come to life.

> So I prophesied as he commanded me, and the breath came into them, and they lived and stood on their feet, an exceedingly great army. (Ezekiel 37:10)

It is in the context of the New Covenant promise of the Spirit that this dramatic vision was given (Ezekiel 36:27). It should come as no surprise that the Hebrew word translated *breath* in Ezekiel's vision is the same word translated *Spirit* in the Scriptures. When the Lord declared that He would put breath in those bones, and bring life, and they would know He is God, He was saying, "I will put my Spirit in you and you shall know Me." When Ezekiel was prophesying to the breath he was prophesying to the Spirit to come from the four winds of the earth and bring life.

Spirit, then, is a word used in the Scriptures that has a very vivid and profound meaning. It means breath, it means wind. Jesus explained to Nicodemus, "The wind blows where it wishes, and you hear its sound, but you do not know where it comes from or where it goes. So it is with everyone who is born of the Spirit" (John 3:8). We witness the wind do all sorts of things—whirling leaves, turning over trees and houses, moving the very landscape of the earth. And when we think about the Spirit, *this* is how we should think about Him: Always in action, invisible, dynamic, and powerful. It is of *this* Spirit that Christ calls our Helper, our Comforter (John 14:26).

The ministry of the Holy Spirit is to mediate the presence of Jesus Christ to us. The Spirit's role is to create and increase our awareness of Jesus in our lives, as well as our dependency on Him. We can do *nothing* apart from Christ, and the Holy Spirit makes us aware of that. Through the agency of the Spirit, Christ is actually present with us. Jesus comforted His disconcerted disciples at the last supper:

> "And I will ask the Father, and he will give you another Helper, to be with you forever, even the Spirit of truth, whom the world cannot receive, because it neither sees him nor knows him. You know him, for he dwells with you and will be in you. I will not leave you as orphans, I will come to you." (John 14:16-18)

Christ would not leave His followers as orphans, but through the Spirit His presence would be known. Jesus dwells within each believer though the presence of the Holy Spirit. This is a covenant promise made by the Lord.

Let us look, now, at how the New Covenant is a "ministry of the Spirit" (2 Corinthians 3:8).

"FROM ONE DEGREE OF GLORY TO ANOTHER…"

We have previously discussed the Biblical concept of *glory*. Humans were created "crowned with glory" (Psalm 8:5), meaning they were formed in the image of God, to reflect His glory. However, when mankind fell in Eden, all were constituted sinners in Adam, and "all have sinned and fall short of the *glory* of God" (Romans 3:23). The image of God has been marred by sin. Christ came to redeem the lost and to bring "many sons to glory" (Hebrews 2:10). Jesus has imparted His life to us through His resurrection. It was the apostle Paul's privilege, then, to reveal a great mystery, which is "Christ in you, the hope of glory" (Colossians 1:27). Our living hope is that now the life of Jesus Christ dwells within every Christian. Now we will build on this concept. We shall see how this concept works itself out practically in our lives and in it find a glimpse of what it means to walk in the Spirit.

Paul, in his letter to the Corinthians, contrasted the glory of the Old Covenant with that of the New Covenant:

> Now if the ministry of death, carved in letters on stone, came with such glory that the Israelites could not gaze at Moses' face because of its glory, which was being brought to an end, will not the ministry of the Spirit have even more glory? For if there was glory in the ministry of

> condemnation, the ministry of
> righteousness must far exceed it in glory.
> Indeed, in this case, what once had glory
> has come to have no glory at all, because
> of the glory that surpasses it. For if what
> was being brought to an end came with
> glory, much more will what is permanent
> have glory. (2 Corinthians 3:7-11)

The Old Covenant did indeed come with glory. The glory of the Old Covenant is symbolically represented by the face of Moses. After Israel had sinned at Sinai and broke their covenant with God by building a golden calf, Moses interceded on their behalf. The Lord agreed to show mercy to His people. It was in this moment that Moses was so captivated by God's presence that he begged the Lord, "Moses said, 'Please show me your glory'" (Exodus 33:18). And God was gracious to His servant! He agreed to hide Moses in the cleft of a rock, and to make His presence pass before Moses and to declare His name to him (Exodus 33:19-23). When Moses came down from the top of Sinai with the stone tablets, his face was shining brightly because he had been with the Lord:

> When Moses came down from Mount
> Sinai, with the two tablets of the
> testimony in his hand as he came down
> from the mountain, Moses did not know
> that the skin of his face shone because he
> had been talking with God. Aaron and all
> the people of Israel saw Moses, and
> behold, the skin of his face shone, and

> they were afraid to come near him. But Moses called to them... The people of Israel came near, and he commanded them all that the Lord had spoken with him in Mount Sinai. And when Moses had finished speaking with them, he put a veil over his face. (Exodus 34:29-31, 32-33)

The people were afraid when they saw how bright Moses' face was. From that time on, Moses would always wear a veil over his face, removing it *only* when he would go to speak with God:

> Whenever Moses went in before the Lord to speak with him, he would remove the veil, until he came out. And when he came out and told the people of Israel what he was commanded, the people of Israel would see the face of Moses, that the skin of Moses' face was shining. And Moses would put the veil over his face again, until he went in to speak with him. (Exodus 34:34-35)

In and out, every time, Moses would take off the veil in the presence of God, would then speak to the camp of Israel, and cover his face afterwards. The glory of the Old Covenant was represented by this shining face of Moses— a face that had to be covered with a veil because of its brightness. And the Scriptures explain that *this* glory was being brought to an end, and the glory of the New

Covenant far exceeded it. In fact, the glory of the New Covenant surpassed the glory of the Old Covenant to such an extent that "what once had glory has come to have no glory at all, because of the glory that surpasses it" (2 Corinthians 3:10). Then the shocking purpose of the veil covering Moses' face is finally revealed:

> Since we have such a hope, we are very bold, not like Moses, who would put a veil over his face so that the Israelites *might not gaze at the outcome of what was being brought to an end.* (2 Corinthians 3:12-13)

Here is *the* scandal of the Old Testament. Moses would always wear a veil because the glory of the law was *fading.* The brightness coming from Moses' face was fleeing from him. The covenant that promised life through obedience brought only death, and was being brought to an end. Now, this symbolism has implications towards those in Jesus Christ.

> But their minds were hardened. For to this day, when they read the old covenant, that same veil remains unlifted, because only through Christ is it taken away. Yes, to this day whenever Moses is read a veil lies over their hearts. (2 Corinthians 3:14-15)

People who live under the law wear veils every day. These veils hide a fading glory, just as the veil of Moses did. The veils are not physical, but symbolic, covering the darkness of heart in men.

The veils that people wear today are all different, but serve the same function. They are facades men use to hide who they *really* are on the inside. Veils come in all forms: pride, false humility, hypersensitivity, frantic religious activity, self-righteousness, self-love, self-isolation, even busyness, just to name a few. These hypocrisies come in many forms, but are all facades people use who are living under the law. While by the law no man will stand before God, one may stand before his peers while hiding behind a veil.

Next we read something magnificent about glory, and sanctification, and true spirituality in Jesus Christ:

> But when one turns to the Lord, the veil is removed. Now the Lord is the Spirit, and where the Spirit of the Lord is, there is freedom. And we all, *with unveiled face, beholding the glory of the Lord, are being transformed into the same image from one degree of glory to another.* For this comes from the Lord who is the Spirit. (2 Corinthians 3:16-18)

Whenever someone turns to the Lord, the veil that covers their heart is removed, for "only through Christ is it taken away" (2 Corinthians 3:14). This removal comes from the very Spirit of God, and brings much freedom. A Christian who walks by the Spirit knows a freedom that the law can never provide.

As noted before, the restored glory we now possess is "Christ in you, the hope of glory" (Colossians 1:27).

However, this glory has not reached its full measure. Even though the life of Christ indwells each believer by the agency of the Holy Spirit, Scripture calls us to work this great salvation out in our own lives (Philippians 2:12-13). How are we to do this? Well, it is a beautiful thing, and it works like this: The success of the New Covenant is because of the Lord's faithfulness to fulfill *both* ends of the covenant. While in the Old Covenant Israel made all the promises and broke every one of them, in the New Covenant God makes *all* the promises that He will be faithful to fulfill. The Lord promises to put His Spirit inside of us, and cause us to live holy and obedient lives. Consequently, our sufficiency in the New Covenant comes *not* from ourselves, but from the Lord: "Not that we are sufficient in ourselves to claim anything as coming from us, but our *sufficiency is from God*" (2 Corinthians 3:5). Christ is the guarantor of a greater covenant. *Christ will be our sufficiency in all things*.

As we look to Jesus to be our sufficiency in all things, we are told that we are being *transformed* from one degree of glory to another. "And we all, with unveiled face, beholding the glory of the Lord, *are being transformed into the same image* from one degree of glory to another (2 Corinthians 3:18). From this we begin to learn to put off the old ways of the flesh, and to "put on the new self, which is being renewed in knowledge after the image of its Creator" (Colossians 3:10). The degree to which we look to Christ for everything is the degree to which we will be transformed into the same image—the very image of Jesus Christ.

While the Old Covenant is symbolically represented by the covered face of Moses, the New Covenant is represented by something far greater, the perfect face of the Jesus Christ:

> For God, who said, "Let light shine out of darkness," has shone in our hearts to give the light of the knowledge of the glory of God *in the face of Jesus Christ*. (2 Corinthians 4:6)

I think the transformation we experience is much like the way that light overcomes darkness. Jesus declared, "I am the light of the world. Whoever follows me will not walk in darkness, but will have the light of life" (John 8:12). Whatever part of our lives we expose to Him *will* begin to be changed. Whatever habits, attitudes, or situations we actively invite the presence of Jesus into will begin to be transformed, as light causes darkness to flee from its presence. This is profound. And all this is found in the face of Jesus Christ, where we see "the light of the knowledge of the glory of God."

How is this applied? Well, let's say you have a certain situation you struggle with. Maybe there is a person in your life that you are trying to show the love of Christ, but you cannot. Jesus commanded, "You shall love your neighbor as yourself" (Matthew 22:39). And no matter how you try, you cannot love this person with a godly love. So what do you do? *You look away to Jesus.* You simply and honestly pray to God, and tell Him everything. Perhaps you say, "Lord, I want to love this person, but for whatever reason I am a very unloving person towards them. I have no patience. I struggle to be kind to them the way You call me to. Will You change my heart? I give this whole situation to You and trust that Christ will be my sufficiency. Lord, I know that I cannot love anyone with the love of Christ, only Jesus can love this someone with the love of Christ. I invite your Son into this situation, and pray You will be faithful to your covenant promises." And do you know what will happen? God will begin to work in this situation powerfully. How do we know God will do this? We know because He has promised in His word to do so.

The process of sanctification will continue throughout our entire lives. The Lord is progressively conforming you to the image of Christ, "until Christ is formed in you" (Galatians 4:19). While we will never be perfect in this life, we must learn to always look to Jesus Christ to be our sufficiency in all things. In this life we will be transformed only from one degree of glory to another. Yet there will come a moment in eternity when the process of sanctification will be complete, and we will perfectly reflect the glory of God. And what is this moment called? *Glorification*.

> For those whom he foreknew he also predestined to be conformed to the image of his Son, in order that he might be the firstborn among many brothers. And those who he predestined he also called, and those whom he called he also justified, and those whom he justified he also glorified. (Romans 8:29-30)

I do not claim to understand everything of what glorification will be like, but I will say that glorification is a thought that makes my heart leap for joy. "Behold! I tell you a mystery. We shall not all sleep, but we shall all be changed, in a moment, in the twinkling of an eye, at the last trumpet" (1 Corinthians 15:51-52). There will be a moment when God will finish His work in us. The apostle John writes, "Beloved, we are God's children now, and we know that when he appears we shall be like him, because we shall see him as he is" (1 John 3:2). When we look to Christ and see Him as He is, then we shall be like Him. I do not know exactly what it will look like, but I think it will be something so wonderful, more wonderful than we could ever imagine or even hope for. "For now we see in a mirror dimly, but then face to face. Now I know in part; then I shall know fully, even as I have been fully known" (1 Corinthians 13:12). Let us be content now, however, with the great inheritance we currently possess in Christ.

TREASURE IN JARS OF CLAY

As the life of Christ dwells within every Christian, we must ask ourselves: How is His life expressed through us? How does the Holy Spirit mediate the presence of Jesus to each child of God? We are given a clue of this when the Scriptures explain, "we have this treasure in jars of clay, to show that the surpassing power belongs to God and not to us" (2 Corinthians 4:7). Every Christian is merely a clay jay. A clay pot does not have value in itself, but is valuable because it can *contain* something. Even the most ordinary jar may hold a king's ransom in treasure. And this is why we have a treasure in clay jars: The treasure *is* the life of Jesus Christ inside each one of us. God hides His treasure inside of jars made from dirt to prove that "the surpassing power belongs to God and not to us."

As the Spirit of God dwells within every Christian, there is a need for the Spirit to be *released*. The breath of God, the Spirit, must breathe through the redeemed soul. Remember that our humanity was created with a threefold composition: body, soul, and spirit (1 Thessalonians 5:23). The Holy Spirit, now united with the human spirit (1 Corinthians 6:17), must so impact the soul as to display the life and character of Christ in each of us. There are several ways that this is accomplished. The apostle Paul prays for the Christians in Ephesus:

> For this reason I bow my knees before the Father, from whom every family in heaven and on earth is named, that according to the riches of his glory he may grant you to be strengthened with power through his Spirit in your inner being, so that Christ may dwell in your hearts through faith—that you, being rooted and grounded in love, may have strength to comprehend with all the saints what is the breadth and length and height and depth, and to know the love of Christ that surpasses knowledge, that you may be filled with all the fullness of God. (Ephesians 3:14-19)

Paul prays for the Ephesians to have strength, not to *do* something, but to *know* something. They need the Spirit to grant them strength in their inner being to know divine truth. And what is it that he prays for them to know? "What is the breadth and length and height and depth, and *to know the love of Christ* that surpasses knowledge" (Ephesians 3:18-19). They need strength to know the love of Jesus Christ. The same is true of every Christian. And what would be the result of *this* kind of knowing? "That Christ may dwell in your hearts through faith... That you may be filled with all the fullness of God" (Ephesians 3:17, 19). Through knowing God's infinite love for them in Christ, the very presence of Jesus would dwell in their hearts. The same is true of us. I am convinced from this passage of one thing: *There is much more of God to be had than we can imagine.* Do you desire to be filled with all the fullness of God? Set yourself to know the love of God in Jesus Christ. This, then, is one way the Spirit affects our souls to mediate the presence of Christ: By illuminating the love of Christ to each of us, the Holy Spirit is manifesting the presence of Jesus in our lives. We are filled with all the fullness of God through a divine awareness of the love of Jesus Christ.

Another way the Holy Spirit expresses Christ's life in us is through brokenness. The Christian life is not free of difficulties. In fact, it is often the trials and suffering that the Spirit uses to make us aware of our dependency on Jesus. The Bible speaks of this when it explains the New Covenant:

> But we have this treasure in jars of clay, to show that the surpassing power belongs to God and not to us. We are afflicted in every way, but not crushed; perplexed, but not driven to despair;

persecute, but not forsaken; struck down, but not destroyed; always carrying in the body the death of Jesus, so that the life of Jesus may be manifested in our bodies. For we who live are always being given over to death for Jesus' sake, so that the life of Jesus might be manifested in our mortal flesh. (2 Corinthians 4:7-11)

God will not allow the Spirit to be restricted in those who have been born of God. If a light is hidden inside of a jar—"we have this treasure in jars of clay"—then the jar *must* be cracked and broken for the light to shine out into the darkness. This process is painful, but a jar must be smashed open before the inner treasure can be exposed. This is what is meant by, "We who live are always being given over to death for Jesus' sake, so that the life of Jesus might be manifested in our mortal flesh" (2 Corinthians 4:11). When we are brought to an end of ourselves the Spirit of Christ will be released.

In the book of Judges God spoke to Gideon and commanded him to whittle his army down to 300 men. "The people with you are too many for me to give the Midianites into their hand, lest Israel boast over me, saying 'My own hand has saved me'" (Judges 7:2). If Gideon's army was too large, Israel would have believed that the surpassing power belonged to them and not to the Lord. Once the army was weak enough, Gideon's men took trumpets and torches that were covered by jars of clay. They surrounded the Midianites at night, and upon Gideon's command they blew their trumpets and *smashed* the jars of clay. It was only when the jars were smashed that the light was exposed. Gideon's tiny army defeated the Midianites, and proved that the surpassing power belonged to God and not to man. The jars speak of brokenness, the light speaks of the life of Christ.

The principle of brokenness is consistent throughout Scripture:

> Count it all joy, my brothers, when you meet trials of various kinds, for you know that the testing of your faith produces steadfastness. And let steadfastness have its full effect, that you may be perfect and complete lacking in nothing. (James 1:2-4)

> More than that, we rejoice in our sufferings, knowing that suffering produces endurance, and endurance produces character, and character produces hope, and hope does not put us to shame, because God's love has been poured into our hearts through the Holy Spirit who has been given to us. (Romans 5:3-5)

The Spirit uses suffering, brokenness, and weaknesses to mediate the presence of Christ to us. Another picture of brokenness is found in the Gospel of Mark: "And as He [Jesus] was at Bethany in the house of Simon the leper, as He was reclining at table, a woman came with an alabaster flask of ointment of pure nard, very costly, and *she broke the flask* and poured it over his head" (Mark 14:3). The pure perfume is symbolic of the Holy Spirit. It was only when the flask was *broken* that the perfume could be poured out and its aroma was allowed to permeate the whole room. Likewise, we are "the aroma of Christ to God among those who are perishing, to one a fragrance of death to death, to the other a fragrance from life to life" (2 Corinthians 2:15-16). It is through adversity, trials, suffering, hardships, and brokenness that the power of Christ is manifest in our lives. "We who live are always being given over to death for Jesus' sake, *so that the life of Jesus might be manifested in our mortal flesh*" (2 Corinthians 4:11). Christians are made continually weaker so that the power of God can rest upon them. May the Holy Spirit be in the midst of our trials, and may He teach us dependence upon Christ through brokenness: "Therefore I will boast all the more gladly in my weaknesses, so that the power of Christ may rest upon me. For the sake of Christ, then I am content with weaknesses, insults, hardships, persecutions, and calamities. *For when I am weak, then I am strong*" (2 Corinthians 12:9-10).

THE FLESH AND THE SPIRIT

In the book of Romans is described the tension between living according to the Spirit or according to the flesh:

> For those who live according to the flesh
> set their minds on the things of the flesh,
> but those who live according to the Spirit
> set their minds on the things of the Spirit.

> To set the mind on the flesh is death, but to set the mind on the Spirit is life and peace. For the mind that is set on the flesh is hostile to God, for it does not submit to God's law; indeed, it cannot. Those who are in the flesh cannot please God. (Romans 8:5-8)

We have grasped what it means for someone to be *in* Adam or *in* Christ. These are *objective* positions every person may possess, dictated by birth or by faith in Christ. Every man's identity is determined by either Adam or Christ. Those who are born naturally are in Adam, and those who have had a second birth are in Christ (John 3:5-6). The flesh and the Spirit are *subjective*, and are a matter or practical experience. Those in Adam can only be in the flesh, for the Spirit of God does not dwell within them (Romans 8:9). They have not had a second birth and the Holy Spirit has not taken up residence within them. Those in Christ, however, can be either in the Spirit or in the flesh.

The apostle Paul's argument in Romans is that it is not enough to be in Christ as a matter of position. "For if you live according to the flesh you will die, but if by the Spirit you put to death the deeds of the body, you will live" (Romans 8:13). If we want to know and experience everything that is objectively true of us in Christ, we must live according to the Spirit. We must walk by the Spirit. If we do not live according to the Spirit we will experience *death*—sin, apathy, darkness, and a lack of passion for the things of God.

In the flesh our lives become a contradiction from

who we are in Christ. It would be like a rich man living in poverty and sickness. While he has the funds to buy and house and see a doctor, he is ignorant of how to do so. Instead, he lives as a beggar in some slum or back alley. So it is with every Christian who does not walk by the Spirit.

Walking by the Spirit is looking to Jesus Christ to be our sufficiency in all things. It is looking to Him to do in us what we cannot do ourselves—allowing Christ to be the fulfillment of the law in us. It is trusting God to do *everything* in us, for apart from Jesus we can to *nothing* (John 15:5). What is the flesh? What does it mean to live according to the flesh? *The flesh is who we are and what we make of ourselves apart from the Spirit of God.* It is our ordinary human nature that does not delight in the things of God. The flesh desires independence from God, not dependence upon Him for all things. It is *not* the same thing as the power of sin. The flesh is *anything* we do out from ourselves, no matter how seemingly good or evil. The flesh operates within the realm of self-effort and human strength. And so the flesh is worthless to God (Romans 8:8).

At any moment a Christian can either be in the flesh or in the Spirit. Those who are in Christ can either be looking to Him for all things (Spirit), or foolishly trying to please God in their own best efforts (flesh). We read these words in Galatians:

> For the desires of the flesh are against the Spirit, and the desires of the Spirit are against the flesh, for these are opposed to each other, to keep you from doing the things you want to do. (Galatians 5:17)

The Spirit and the flesh are two forces that oppose each other. They are, as it were, at war with each other. The natural desires of the flesh are against the Holy Spirit, and the supernatural desires of the Spirit contradict those of the flesh, to keep us from doing what we want.

Now, we must ask ourselves: What is it that we would *naturally* want to do? We would do something by our own efforts, in our own strength, and *not* in dependence on the Spirit. This was our habit before coming to Christ, and it is our natural tendency even after coming to Christ. Unless the Spirit of God *supernaturally* intervenes, we desire the flesh. Walking in the Spirit is what we do when the desires of the Spirit are *stronger* than the desires of the flesh.

The Old Covenant is the *default* mode by which people naturally live under, even Christians. While the law is natural to us, the gospel must be preached into us. The New Covenant is a "ministry of the Spirit" (2 Corinthians 3:8). We experience the fulfillment of the prophecy Ezekiel spoke of whenever we walk in the Spirit of God. However, the Old Covenant is a "ministry of death" (2 Corinthians 3:7). The moment we walk according to the flesh we place ourselves under the Old Covenant and experience death: "For those who live according to the flesh set their minds on the things of the flesh, but those who live according to the Spirit set their minds on the things of the Spirit. To set the mind on the flesh is death, but to set the mind on the Spirit is life and peace" (Romans 8:5-6). And the solution to the flesh always comes by the Spirit. "But I say, walk by the Spirit, and you will not gratify the desires of the flesh" (Galatians 5:16).

The Spirit entering our lives and overcoming the flesh came by the person and work of Jesus Christ:

> There is therefore now no condemnation for those who are in Christ Jesus. For the law of the Spirit of life has set you free in Christ Jesus from the law of sin and death. For God has done what the law, weakened by the flesh, could not do. By sending his own Son in the likeness of sinful flesh and for sin, he condemned sin in the flesh, in order that the righteous requirement of the law might be fulfilled in us, who walk not according to the flesh but according to the Spirit. (Romans 8:1-4)

The law was not a bad thing. "So the law is holy, and the commandment is holy and righteous and good" (Romans 7:12). However, the law had no power for salvation. It could not save us. The problem of the law was what it had to work with—the flesh. The law was "weakened by the flesh," and commandments carved in stone could never bring righteousness and salvation. However, God did in Jesus Christ what the law could never do: When Jesus died on the cross, God condemned sin in the flesh, for it was on the cross that Christ was made sin on our behalf (2 Corinthians 5:21). And all of this had a grand purpose: "He condemned sin in the flesh, in order that the righteous requirement of the law might be fulfilled in us, *who walk not according to the flesh but according to the Spirit*" (Romans 8:3-4). The Lord condemned sin in the flesh, in order that Christ might fulfill the law in us, who live according to the Spirit of God.

Now, this has practical implications and enlightens a passage we have already explored:

> O foolish Galatians! Who has bewitched you? It was before your eyes that Jesus Christ was publicly portrayed as crucified. Let me ask you only this: Did you receive the Spirit by works of the law or by hearing with faith? Are you so foolish? Having begun by the Spirit, are you now being perfected by the flesh? (Galatians 3:1-3)

There are several points made in this passage. First, we received the Spirit on the basis of faith alone. We did *not* receive the Holy Spirit through works of the law or by any doing on our own part. The new birth was the result of the free work of the God (John 3:5-6). Then we are presented with a rhetorical question: "Having begun by the Spirit, are you now being perfected by the flesh?" (Galatians 3:3). The obvious answer to this question is no! Spiritual growth does not come by works of the law or the flesh. It only comes by the Spirit of God. Growth in grace comes by the same way as the new birth—by faith in Jesus Christ and the working of the Holy Spirit.

Tragically, many Christians seek growth through incorrect means. Although they are likely quite sincere, they are foolishly trying to be perfected by the flesh instead of faith in Christ. "It is the Spirit who gives life; the flesh is of no avail" (John 6:63). We can do many things which on the outside appear to be spiritual—Bible study, fasting, prayer, and so forth—but if these are done are a work of the *flesh*, they profit nothing. All endeavors must be done by faith, trusting in the Spirit to give life. Apart from Christ we can do nothing (John 15:5). We must walk by faith and trust Jesus Christ to be our sufficiency in all things.

The book of Romans continues by illustrating the dynamic between the flesh and the Spirit:

> For those who live according to the flesh set their minds on the things of the flesh, but those who live according to the Spirit set their minds on the things of the Spirit. To set the mind on the flesh is death, but to set the mind on the Spirit is life and peace. For the mind that is set on the flesh is hostile to God, for it does not submit to God's law; indeed, it cannot. Those who are in the flesh cannot please God. (Romans 8:5-8)

The flesh profits nothing, to set the mind on it is death. The Spirit gives life. Those who are according to the flesh will, by *necessity*, be minding the things of the flesh. They will be producing the fruit of the flesh. Those who are according to the Spirit *will* be minding the Spirit. The Spirit will be producing fruit in their lives. *And those who are in the flesh cannot please God.* No matter how sincere one may be, or how good their intentions, or even how religious their pursuit, there is *nothing* in the flesh that pleases God. It is impossible. That which pleases God is born of the Spirit of God, and comes by faith in Jesus Christ.

> You, however, are not in the flesh but in the Spirit, if in fact the Spirit of God dwells in you. Anyone who does not have the Spirit of Christ does not belong to him. But if Christ is in you, although the body is dead because of sin, the Spirit is life because of righteousness. If the Spirit of him who raised Jesus from the dead dwells in you, he who raised Christ Jesus from the dead will also give life to your mortal bodies through his Spirit who dwells in you. (Romans 8:9-11)

Those who belong to Jesus have the Holy Spirit inside of them by authority of Christ's exaltation at the right hand of the Father (Acts 2:33). The Spirit is mediating to us Christ our life. These are not mere theological abstractions, this is life itself. This means the power of His resurrected life is always present and available, mighty to save. *Are you living according to His life that dwells within you?* We are urged in Galatians, "If we live by the Spirit, let us also walk by the Spirit" (Galatians 5:25). Jesus Christ is present. He wants us to find our rest, our strength, our life, everything in Him.

WALKING BY THE SPIRIT

We have been united with Jesus Christ in His death

and resurrection, and because of this we are commanded to present ourselves to God as instruments of righteousness, as those who have been brought from death to life (Romans 6:13). Through this process the Spirit is conforming us to the image of Christ. Thus Jesus is given access to our mind, will, and emotions, and allowed to manifest His life in us. Consequently, presenting ourselves to God *leads* to walking in the Spirit.

Looking to Jesus to be our sufficiency in all things and walking by the Spirit, then, are one and the same. "Now the Lord is the Spirit, and where the Spirit of the Lord is, there is freedom. And we all, with unveiled face, beholding the glory of the Lord, are being transformed into the same image from one degree of glory to another. *For this comes from the Lord who is the Spirit*" (2 Corinthians 3:17-18). Just as the Holy Spirit moved through the valley of dry bones in Ezekiel's vision, so too is He sweeping through our lives. The Spirit makes real to us the tangible and practical terms of the resurrection of Christ, and mediates to us the presence of Jesus. Walking by the Spirit means we trust the Holy Spirit to do in us what we cannot do ourselves. If we desire to experience all that is true of us in Christ, we must learn to walk by the Spirit.

How are we to know whether or not we are walking in the Spirit? "But I say, walk by the Spirit, and you will not gratify the desires of the flesh. For the desires of the flesh are against the Spirit, and the desires of the Spirit are against flesh, for these are opposed to each other, to keep you from doing the things you want to do" (Galatians 5:16-17). Walking by the Spirit is what we do when the desires of the Spirit are stronger than the desires of the flesh. Jesus taught His disciples:

"You will recognize them by their fruits.
Are grapes gathered from thorn bushes,
or figs from thistles? So, every healthy
tree bears good fruit, but the diseased tree
bears bad fruit. A healthy tree cannot
bear bad fruit, nor can a diseased tree
bear good fruit. Every tree that does not
bear good fruit is cut down and thrown
into the fire. Thus you will recognize
them by their fruits." (Matthew 7:16-20)

Here is an important spiritual principle: *A good tree cannot
bear bad fruit, nor can a bad tree bear good fruit.* At any moment
if you are looking away to Jesus and are according to the
Spirit, good fruit *will* be produced in your life by the Spirit
of God. It must be so. Those who are according to the
Spirit are minding the things of the Spirit (Romans 8:5).
They will be experiencing the fulfillment of the prophecy
spoken through Ezekiel, "And I will put my Spirit within
you, and cause you to walk in my statutes and be careful to
obey my rules" (Ezekiel 36:27).

Tell me, are you allowing the holy breath of God to
breathe through you? Are you opening your heart wide to
allow the Spirit to manifest the life of Christ in you? "And
he said to me, 'Son of man, can these bones live?' And I
answered, 'O Lord God, you know'" (Ezekiel 37:3).
However, at any moment you take your eyes off of Jesus
Christ you will be according to the flesh, producing only
bad fruit again.

From this we shoulder understand something,
namely, it is the fruit *of the* Spirit being produced in the life

of the believer, *not* the fruit of the Christian. Whatever good fruit that is produced in the life of a Christian is the handiwork of the Spirit of God.

The fruit of the Spirit is produced in the soul (mind, will, emotions). For instance, God will transform the human mind, giving us the mind of Christ (1 Corinthians 2:16). The Spirit is putting down anything that keeps us from the true knowledge of God: "We destroy arguments and every lofty opinion raised against the knowledge of God, and *take every thought captive to obey Christ*" (2 Corinthians 10:5). Likewise, we are urged in Romans: "Do not be conformed to this world, but *be transformed by the renewal of your mind*, that by testing you may discern what is the will of God, what is good and acceptable and perfect" (Romans 12:2).

How is your thought-life? What do you spend your time thinking about? The Holy Spirit will take captive corrupt, sinful thoughts which are in rebellion to the true knowledge of God. Likewise, if we set our minds upon God's truth, the Bible, the Spirit will illuminate that truth to renew our minds and to conform us to the image of Jesus Christ.

In the same manner, the Lord wants to transform our emotions. Emotions are not to be an end in themselves, but should rightly be drawn *toward* something, namely, the majesty and excellency of God. Consequently, much of the fruit of the Spirit manifests itself as emotions: "The fruit of the Spirit is love, joy, peace, patience, kindness, goodness, faithfulness, gentleness, self-control..." (Galatians 5:22-23). Now, while we must not reduce the work of the Spirit to an emotional appeal, the Spirit *does* transform our emotions. How are you feeling today? Are you depressed, bored, and indifferent to the things of God? Or are you looking past yourself, to the risen Savior, to have a sense of the excellence of the Divine? "To see the mind on the flesh is death, but to set the mind on the Spirit is life and peace" (Romans 8:6). When you walk in the Spirit, He will take captive your heart and produce godly fruit in your life.

God also wants to affect the will of the Christian. Before we came to Christ, our wills were enslaved to the power of sin. However, after coming to Christ, we were set free from sin. Now, we can either present ourselves to God or yield the members of our bodies to sin. Yet we must always remember that whoever we present our members to, we *will* become their slave. Human beings were made to be mastered. "Now the Lord is the Spirit, and where the Spirit of the Lord is, there is *freedom*" (2 Corinthians 3:17). What sort of decisions are you making today? Are you experiencing self-control, or are you in bondage to sin? Paul writes:

> Therefore, my beloved, as you have always obeyed, so now, not only in my presence but much more now in my absence, work out your salvation with fear and trembling, for it is God who works in you, both to will and for his good pleasure. (Philippians 2:12-13)

The mighty Spirit of God is working in us, to affect our wills for His good pleasure. If we walk in the Spirit we will know the sweetest freedom in Christ.

May our hearts be open wide to the ministry of the Holy Spirit. The life of Jesus Christ indwells each of us through the agency of the Spirit. My prayer is that you would learn to put off the old ways of the flesh and to allow the Spirit of God to be released in your life. "If we life by the Spirit, let us also walk by the Spirit" (Galatians 5:25).

CHAPTER 08 – BEARING THE CROSS

"If anyone would come after me, let him deny himself and take up his cross daily and follow me." (Luke 9:23)

TRUE SPIRITUALITY

Listen:

Everything that we have studied so far has brought us to a single question: What is true spirituality? Or, stated another way: How do we live the authentic Christian life? The answer to this question means everything. The apostle Paul explained the nature of true spirituality in his letter to the Galatians:

> I have been crucified with Christ. It is no longer I who live, but Christ who lives in me. And the life I now live in the flesh I live by faith in the Son of God, who loved me and gave himself up for me.

(Galatians 2:20)

This verse describes, again, how those in Jesus Christ have been baptized into Him, His death, burial, and resurrection. The life that dwells within each Christian is the very life of Jesus Christ. Four words can summarize this verse into the essence of true spirituality: *Not I, but Christ.* The Scriptures declare, "For you have died, and your life is hidden with Christ in God. When *Christ who is your life* appears, then you also will appear with him in glory" (Colossians 3:3-4). These are objective facts that are true of every child of God; regardless of their wavering experiences and shifting feelings—all of us have our lives hidden with Christ in God.

And yet we must be honest with ourselves here. Do we *really* see the life of Jesus Christ made manifest in the church? Is the very life of Jesus being made manifest in *you* as it ought? The church is supposed to be the aroma of Christ to a dead and dying world (2 Corinthians 2:15-16). But I fear people do not smell Him when they are near us. If the Christian life *is* Christ, one might argue that Christians should display the life of Jesus automatically. At least that is what one might think. However, the teaching of Scripture is straightforward that this is *not* how the Christian life works. Jesus taught His disciples a spiritual principle and the way of true spirituality:

> "Truly, truly, I say to you, unless a grain of wheat falls into the earth and dies, it remains alone; but if it dies, it bears much fruit." (John 12:14)

Here is an important spiritual principle, one that applies *both* to Jesus' death and to our practical experience. Christ spoke these words as the time was approaching for His glorification (John 12:22). Remember, it was through His glorification that the Spirit would be gifted to His church (John 7:38-39). Through the Spirit of Christ dwelling within His people, rivers of living water would flow out of their hearts. *But first Jesus had to die.* "Unless a grain of wheat falls into the earth and dies, it remains alone." And through His resurrection and glorification new life would come. "But if it dies, it bears much fruit." The same is true of our own lives. And here is why there is so little fruitfulness in the church today: We do not die to ourselves. The only way a tiny grain of wheat can bear fruit is to first fall into the earth and die. Jesus similarly spoke:

> And he said to all, "If anyone would come after me, let him deny himself and take up his cross daily and follow me. For whoever would save his life will lose it, but whoever loses his life for my sake will save it." (Luke 9:23-24)

We are called to die *every day*, even though we have already been crucified with Jesus Christ, once for all time. What we need to understand from this is that there is a *practical outworking* of spiritual truth in our lives. All Biblical truth is applied by faith. This is the consistent teaching of Scripture. For example, although we who have been brought near to God by the blood, we are then told to continually draw near to Him (Hebrews 10:19-20, 22). Or even though we have been clothed with Christ (Galatians 3:27), we are told to "put on Christ" (Romans 13:14). And although we have become one spirit with the Lord (1 Corinthians 6:17), we are also continually told to be filled with the Holy Spirit (Ephesians 5:18). And the apostle Paul also writes in Colossians, "For you have died, and your life is hidden with Christ in God... Put to death therefore what is earthly in you" (Colossians 3:3, 5). So the man who *has* died is commanded to be given over to death again and again.

Two things must be understood before one can properly know how to bear the cross. These two points will lay the groundwork for understanding this vital passage. First, before Christ ever spoke about His death on the cross, or called His followers to die every day, Jesus first convinced the disciples as to whom He was as a *person*. The parallel passages to Luke 9:23-24 are found in Matthew 16:24 and Mark 8:34. Prior to each account is given the moment when Peter confessed that Jesus was the Christ:

> Now when Jesus came into the district of Caesarea Philippi, He asked His disciples, "Who do people say that the Son of Man is?" And they said, "Some say John the Baptist, others say Elijah, and others Jeremiah or one of the prophets." He said to them, "But who do you say that I am?" Simon Peter replied, "You are the Christ, the Son of the living God." (Matthew 16:13-16)

It was only after Peter's confession that Christ then explained to His disciples that He came to earth in order to die:

> From that time Jesus began showing his disciples that he must go to Jerusalem and suffer many things from the elders and chief priests and scribes, and be killed, and on the third day raised. (Matthew 16:21)

It was only "from that time," the time after the disciples finally understood that Jesus was the Christ that He then explained to them how He must die for their sins and rise from the dead. The same is true of us. Until we are convinced of who Jesus Christ is as a person, we will see *nothing* in His death. And flesh and blood cannot reveal such things. The Spirit must illuminate to us that Jesus is the Christ, the Son of God. Has He convinced you that Jesus is the Son of God, and is able to do through you immeasurably more than you can imagine? We must know the person before we understand His work. This is an important point, one that should be kept firmly in our minds as we explore bearing our crosses, for we shall revisit this idea later.

The second point to notice about Jesus' command for us to die daily is that it is patterned after His own death:

> And he strictly charged and commanded them to tell this to no one, saying, "The Son of Man must suffer many things and be *rejected* by the elders and chief priests

> and scribes, and be *killed*, and on the third
> day be *raised*." And He said to all, "If
> anyone would come after me, let him *deny*
> himself and *take up his cross daily* and *follow*
> *me*." (Luke 9:21-23)

The order that Jesus followed (rejected, killed, raised) is the *same pattern* that we follow as well. Christ, as the captain of our faith, has given us the ultimate example. Jesus was rejected, killed, and raised; if we would come after Him, we must walk the same lonely path: denying ourselves (rejected), taking up our crosses daily (killed) and following Him (raised).

What of ourselves is to be put to death every day? It is our natural life—the flesh. Remember, the flesh is *not* the same thing as our old Adamic nature, which was included in the death of Jesus. As a matter of *position* we are no longer in Adam but are in Christ. That death was once-for-all, included in the crucifixion of Christ. This position remains true no matter whether we are living according to the flesh or the Spirit. Thus walking in the Spirit or the flesh is a matter of *practice*. Again, the flesh is what we are and what we make of ourselves apart from the Spirit of God. We are living according to the flesh when the desires of the flesh are greater than the desires of the Spirit. And God has pronounced a death sentence upon the flesh.

When we speak of the natural life, it is called the *natural* life because it stands in antithesis to a different kind of life, the *supernatural* life. The supernatural life is the Divine life operating within us. The supernatural life is that which is of God; the natural life is that which is of the flesh. In broad terms the flesh is any form of self-effort, whether one is purposefully breaking the law of God, or they are sincerely trying to live for God in their own strength. All of the flesh, the natural life, is worthless to God. "Those who are in the flesh *cannot* please God" (Romans 8:8). In the flesh even our best righteousness are as filthy rags to Him. We must learn to deny ourselves, to take up our crosses and to each day allow the cross to "put to death therefore what is earthly in you" (Colossians 3:5), and to follow Jesus.

"LET HIM DENY HIMSELF..."

Jesus taught His disciples, "If anyone would come after me, let him deny himself" (Luke 9:23). Christ's command for us to deny ourselves is a hard phrase to swallow. His words cut through everything and go down to the most practical moments of everyday life. We should be careful not to romanticize His words or reduce them to mere abstractions. We cannot take this command lightly because, in reality, it is asking everything of us. If the call to deny ourselves ever seems easy, then we do not understand what Christ is really asking of us. We ought to look at the moment of temptation that Adam and Eve faced in the garden:

> But the serpent said to the woman, "You will not surely die. For God knows that when you eat of it your eyes will be opened, and you will be like God, knowing good and evil." So when the

> woman saw that the tree was good for
> food, and that it was a delight to the eyes,
> and that the tree was to be desired to
> make one wise, she took its fruit and ate,
> and she also gave some to her husband
> who was with her, and he ate. (Genesis
> 3:4-6)

Let's face this passage with a bit of honesty. When Satan
tempted Eve, there had to have been something in her that
wanted to be like God. The fruit of the tree looked good
and delighted her eyes, and she desired to become like
God. The same is true of each of us. We desire to be the
ruler of our own lives and the center of our own universe.
Consequently, the world we live in is one that refuses to
deny the self *anything*. And the flesh delights in being
accepted by a world that is in rebellion against its Creator.
Our natural self *wants* to be dominated by pride and
possessions. The apostle Paul writes of this world:

> But understand this, that in the last days
> there will come times of difficulty. For
> people will be lovers of self, lovers of
> money, proud, arrogant, abusive,
> disobedient to their parents, ungrateful,
> unholy, heartless, unappeasable,
> slanderous, without self-control, brutal,
> not loving good, treacherous, reckless,
> swollen with conceit, lovers of pleasure
> rather than lovers of God, having the
> appearance of godliness, but denying its
> power. (2 Timothy 3:1-5)

The "last days" mentioned in this passage are the span of years from Christ's ascension until His second coming. We are in the last days, we have been in the last days for some time now, and we will be in the last days until Jesus returns with a sword to strike down the nations. Yet I think things will get worse the closer we get to His return. The people described here are lovers of themselves, they love money and pleasure, they are proud and arrogant, without self-control, and are unappeasable in all things. Yet in the midst of all this the Scriptures declare that *a person can retain an appearance of godliness, all while denying its power.* That is the state of much of the church today. Many professing Christians have a form of godliness on the surface, but no real power or true spirituality in Jesus Christ. They love the self and believe that God is there primarily for their own happiness. They deny the power of God and not themselves! And yet I say this with a bit of caution, because I know that I myself could easily become a person like this. With the culture we live in, the deceitfulness of heart and subtleness of the flesh, any one of us could become a lover of self. And so we must not take the call to deny ourselves lightly.

The ways of the flesh are subtle. While our natural selves desire to be at the center of our lives—the throne that rightfully belongs to Jesus—the flesh can still be very religious as long as it is allowed to survive. Most days it is not as if I turn my back on Christ and live in rebellion, but I am more devious than that. I will try to follow Jesus all while *not* denying myself. Christ said, "If anyone would come after me, let him deny himself" (Luke 9:23). If anyone wants to follow Jesus Christ, he *must* deny himself.

He cannot do one and not the other. The heartbeat of every regenerate Christian certainly desires Christ and wants to walk with Him daily. However, the natural life always wants a little left over for the self. Oh, we will give the Lord what we think He commands, while always holding on to a tiny hope that maybe we will have a little left over at the end of the day. *We are not denying ourselves.* To truly deny ourselves is to not allow the flesh *any* hope of having anything left over for the self at the end of the day. If we do not *first* deny ourselves, then the cross will not be able to do its work in our lives.

"TAKE UP HIS CROSS…"

Jesus taught His disciples, "If anyone would come after me, let him deny himself and take up his cross daily" (Luke 9:23). Here is the command to die to ourselves every day. I would like to explore the story of Saul, the first king of Israel, in order to prove how wicked the flesh is and the necessity for it to be put to death daily. The natural talents of Saul would cause anyone to believe that he possessed all the necessary gifts to be a great king. However, it was only a short time after his anointing that he was disqualified as king and rejected by the Lord. Why?

We read that after Saul was anointed king, the Lord gave him a strict command through the prophet Samuel:

> And Samuel said to Saul, "The Lord sent me to anoint you king over his people Israel; now therefore listen to the words of the Lord. Thus says the Lord of hosts,

> 'I have noted what Amalek did to Israel in
> opposing them on the way when they
> came up out of Egypt. Now go and strike
> Amalek and devote to destruction all that
> they have. Do not spare them, but kill
> both man and woman, child and infant,
> ox and sheep, camel and donkey." (1
> Samuel 15:1-3)

Saul was commanded to destroy all the people of Amalek. Amalek was the grandson of Esau, the brother of Jacob. Jacob wrestled with God and his name was changed to Israel—thus Jacob was the head of the nation of Israel. Esau and his descendants, however, are a symbol or type of the flesh. During the time that Israel fled Egypt the Amalekites came and attacked Israel from the rear (Exodus 17:8-13). The Lord declared His judgment upon Amalek for his wickedness:

> Then the Lord said to Moses, "Write this
> as a memorial in a book and recite it in
> the ears of Joshua, that I will utterly blot
> out the memory of Amalek from under
> the heaven." And Moses built an altar and
> called the name of it, The Lord is my
> banner, saying, "A hand upon the throne
> of the Lord! *The Lord will have war with
> Amalek from generation to generation.*"
> (Exodus 17:14-16)

Long before Saul became king of Israel, the Lord declared that He would wipe the Amalekites from the face of the earth. And now it was King Saul's time to be obedient to what the Lord had spoken. Would Saul obey the command of the Lord?

> And Saul defeated the Amalekites from Havilah as far as Shur, which is east of Egypt. And he took Agag the king of the Amalekites alive and devoted to destruction all the people with the edge of the sword. But Saul and the people spared Agag and the best of the sheep and of the oxen and of the fattened calves and the lambs, and all that was good, and would not utterly destroy them. All that was despised and worthless they devoted to destruction. (1 Samuel 15:7-9)

Instead of destroying *all* of the Amalekites as God had commanded, Saul allowed the king to live along with the choicest livestock. King Saul gave only a *partial* obedience. And here is what the Lord thought of Saul's obedience: "The word of the Lord came to Samuel; 'I regret that I have made Saul king, for he has turned back from me and has not performed my commandments'" (1 Samuel 15:10-11). When Samuel finally came to Saul, the king thought that he had done a great service to the Lord. By sparing king Agag and the best livestock of the Amalekites, Saul foolishly believed that the Lord would be pleased with his decision:

> And Samuel came to Saul, and Saul said to him, "Blessed be you to the Lord. I

198

> have performed the commandment of the Lord." And Samuel said, "What then is this bleating of the sheep in my ears and the lowing of the oxen I hear?" Saul said, "They have brought them from the Amalekites, for the people spared the best of the sheep and of the oxen to sacrifice to the Lord your God, and the rest we have devoted to destruction." (1 Samuel 15:13-15)

What was Saul's error? He tried to decide for himself what was good and what was bad in the Amalekites. He did not understand that there was *nothing* in the Amalekites that pleased the Lord. Now, here is the lesson we must see from this: The same principle is true of the flesh. *All that is of the flesh is worthless to God.* While the flesh not only manifests itself in evil deeds, it can also perform many acts that on the surface appear good, even righteous and spiritual. The Pharisees were able to live externally pure lives in the flesh, but was Christ ever impressed by their efforts? Jesus declared to them, "Woe to you, scribes and Pharisees, hypocrites! For you are like whitewashed tombs, which outwardly appear beautiful, but within are full of dead people's bones and all uncleanness" (Matthew 27:23). By outward appearances they were very beautiful, but inside were full of dead things. That is the religion of the flesh. "Those who are in the flesh cannot please God" (Romans 8:8). We must allow the Spirit of God to put to death everything that is of the natural life.

On any given day, we may believe that we are doing quite well and that God should be pleased with our efforts.

Perhaps we have been reading our Bibles more, or are attending church more frequently, or tithing more, or whatever. However, all of these things we can easily do in the power of the flesh. The Bible speaks of abandoning confidence in the flesh in order to gain Christ (Philippians 3:3-7). We must not be like Saul, foolishly deciding what is good and bad in something that the Lord declares to be *all* bad. All of the flesh is under a sentence of death. I will say it again: All self-effort is under a death sentence from God. We must deny ourselves and allow the Spirit to use the cross to daily kill the natural life.

THE SPIRIT'S WORK IN DEATH

Dying to ourselves is *not* something we do in our own efforts but is a work that the Spirit of God does within us. The Scriptures declare, "For if you live according to the flesh you will die, but if *by the Spirit* you put to death the deeds of the body, you will live" (Romans 8:13). *It is by the Spirit that the flesh is crucified daily.* A man cannot nail himself to his own cross. If we try to put to death the ways of the flesh by any other means that the Spirit we will fail. "For the desires of the flesh are against the Spirit, and the desires of the Spirit are against the flesh" (Galatians 5:17). It is the Spirit that opposes and kills the flesh, and as we deny ourselves we must look away to God to do this work within us.

It is the Spirit of Christ that dwells within each one of us and has made His home within us. All other means of death are in vain! The apostle Paul warned the Christians in Colossae:

> If with Christ you died to the elemental spirits of the world, why, as if you were still alive in the world, do you submit to regulations—"Do not handle, Do not taste, Do not touch" (referring to things that all perish as they are used)— according to human precepts and teachings? These have indeed an appearance of wisdom in promoting self-made religion and asceticism and severity to the body, *but are of no value in stopping the indulgence of the flesh.* (Colossians 2:20-23)

We have been included with Jesus Christ in His historical death and are also called to die to ourselves daily. Why then do we presume to live before God again? The apostle Paul admits that there is an *appearance* of wisdom in this form of self-made religion, but it has zero value in stopping the flesh. It is only the Spirit working death in us that can bring resurrection life. Sadly, so much of what is preached from the pulpits today is this same form of false spirituality that tries to reform the flesh to live before God again. They will preach lists of things to do for a better, more fulfilled life, and it has an *appearance* of wisdom. But if it goes against the means that God has ordained to bring life, it is worthless. We must die to live, and this is a work of the Holy Spirit. "For if you live according to the flesh you will die, but if *by the Spirit* you put to death the deeds of the body, you will live" (Romans 8:13).

When something dies it loses all of its strength, power, and abilities. When the Spirit puts to death the natural life, it means we are given over to the supernatural life—the very life of Jesus Christ—for His purposes. Dying to ourselves doesn't mean that we are perfect, or that the power of sin is annihilated (1 John 1:8). It means that the ways of the flesh are being put to death in us so that the presence of Christ can then shine through us. "For we who live are always being given over to death for Jesus' sake, so that the life of Jesus also may be manifested in our mortal flesh" (2 Corinthians 4:11). In effect, we are putting off the flesh and putting on Christ (Romans 13:14). All this is a work that the Spirit is doing in us.

Those who have been raised with Christ are called to put to death the deeds of the flesh (Colossians 3:1-5). If we allow the Spirit of God to do this work within us, we will live. However, if we foolishly try to only reform the flesh and to make it live before God again, we will die. We must deny ourselves, and allow the Spirit to work death in us to kill the flesh and its desires.

"AND FOLLOW ME…"

Jesus taught His disciples, "If anyone would come after me, let him deny himself and take up his cross daily and follow me" (Luke 9:23). He once warned His followers about the cost of being His disciple and the necessity of dying to ourselves. Jesus explained that if we do not bear our own cross we *cannot* be His disciples:

> "Whoever does not bear his own cross
> and come after me cannot be my disciple.
> For which of you, desiring to build a
> tower, does not first sit down and count

the cost, whether he has enough to complete it? Otherwise, when he has laid a foundation and is not able to finish, all who see it begin to most him, saying, 'This man began to build and was not able to finish.'" (Luke 14:27-30)

When we die to ourselves, we die to *everything*. We have no future plans. We are not coming to Christ to make our lives a little happier, a little better. We do not follow Jesus in order to have healthier families. *He means to bring us to an end of ourselves.* The man who hates living his own life will find a new one in Jesus Christ. He spoke, "If anyone comes to me and does not hate his own father and mother and wife and children and brothers and sisters, yes, and even his own life, he cannot be my disciple. Whoever does not bear his own cross and come after me cannot be my disciple" (Luke 14:26-27). Let us be honest: There is a *huge* cost in dying to ourselves. When we deny ourselves, take up our cross daily, and follow Jesus, we are not doing a little thing. We are saying *no* to being dominated by the self and by the things of this world. From a worldly perspective, this costs *everything*. And so Jesus warns us to carefully count this cost. The cross is not there to make your life a little better. It is there to kill you. It means to bring you to nothing. And cross bearing is necessary for being a disciple of Christ.

Jesus likened bearing the cross to a man building a tower. The builder must be careful to count the cost, for if he began to build his tower and could not finish it, he would be mocked as a fool. In a city near where I live, a man wanted to build a great a tower filled with condos and downtown shops and all sorts of extravagance. He began building his giant tower by digging a deep pit. Yet shortly after construction began, the builder went bankrupt. Years later (as I am currently writing this), the failed tower remains. Makeshift walls have been erected to hide the massive eyesore. But if you look closely, you can see everything: The gaping hole, the metal rods coming out of the dirt, the dead machinery lying motionless amongst the abandoned construction. It is easy for a Christian who will not die to themselves to become like that, like a dead machine, caught up in a cold and distant world that judges everything by binges and profit margins. That is what we become when we choose to live our own lives and not to die: "For whoever would save his life will lose it" (Luke 9:24). The natural self always seeks to be satisfied and alive, all because it thinks the cost of death to be much too great.

Yet there is another cost. Yes, the world and the flesh call Christ's command for death to be far too high. "He is asking for too much," they say. This is the world's perspective. However, we are not citizens of the world but are citizens of heaven (Philippians 3:20). We need the Divine perspective on things. There is *another* cost, one that happens when a Christian does *not* die to themselves: "Whoever loses his life for my sake will save it" (Luke 9:24). If we choose to live our own lives and not to die to ourselves it will cost us *everything*, because Jesus Christ has become to us all things. This is the Divine perspective, the perspective the apostle Paul wrote about to the Philippians:

But whatever gain I had, I counted

as loss for the sake of Christ. Indeed, I count everything as loss because of the surpassing worth of knowing Christ Jesus my Lord. For his sake I have suffered the loss of all things and count them as rubbish, in order that I may gain Christ and be found in him, not having a righteousness of my own that comes from the law, but that which comes through faith in Christ, the righteousness from God that depends on faith—that I may know him and the power of his resurrection, and may share his sufferings, becoming like him in his death, that by any means possible I may attain the resurrection from the dead. (Philippians 3:7-11)

Whatever things were gain before (and Paul is speaking here of boasting in the flesh), those things are loss for the sake of Jesus Christ. All things pale in comparison and fade into gray when seen against the infinite splendor of merely knowing Jesus, and being found in Him, and being clothed with His righteousness.

When we die to ourselves what we gain is the resurrection life of Christ being made progressively manifest in our mortal bodies. His life is mediated to us by the agency of the Holy Spirit. The Spirit is killing us and bringing us to an end of ourselves, so that the indwelling life of Christ may flow through us. "For we who live are always being given over to death for Jesus' sake, so that the life of Jesus may be manifested in our mortal flesh" (2 Corinthians 4:11). Dying to ourselves day by day, moment by moment is essential to discipleship. It unleashes the Spirit of Christ to work in and through our lives. This is the exact idea given in Romans when we are told to "present your bodies as a living sacrifice, holy and acceptable to God, which is your spiritual worship" (Romans 12:1). We are to climb upon the altar and become living sacrifices to God. The Spirit will then work death in us so that Jesus Christ will be manifest. However, at any moment we can choose to get off of the altar and start living our own lives again, according to the flesh, exerting self-effort for things we know to be evil as well as things we believe to be good. But Jesus warned us, "For whoever would save his life will lose it, but whoever loses his life for my sake will save it" (Luke 9:24).

Remember Peter's great confession? Whenever we reflect upon dying to ourselves, we must always be conscious of who Jesus is as a person. He is the Christ, the Son of God. He is able to do immeasurably more with our lives than we could ever dream or imagine. This is because when we die to ourselves the life of Christ comes alive in us. *And we are complete in Christ*:

> As you therefore have received Christ Jesus the Lord, so walk in him, rooted and built up in him and established in the faith, as you have been taught, abounding in it with thanksgiving. Beware lest anyone cheat you through philosophy and empty deceit, according to the tradition of men, according to the basic principles of the world, and not according to Christ. For in him dwells all the fullness of the

> Godhead bodily, and *you are complete in him*,
> who is the head of all principality and
> power. (Colossians 2:6-10)

Will you walk in Him? Will you allow the Spirit to bring you to and end of yourself? Everything we will ever possess in Jesus Christ we have right now (We are complete in Him!). There is no hidden secret in Christianity, no next level, and nothing needs to be added. Jesus will be our sufficiency in all things if we look away from ourselves (deny), die daily to everything that is of the flesh (take up the cross), and look away to Him (follow Jesus). This is true spirituality in Jesus Christ.

CHAPTER 09 – ABIDING IN CHRIST

"I am the vine; you are the branches. Whoever abides in me and I in him, he it is that bears much fruit, for apart from me you can do nothing." (John 15:5)

THE TRUE VINE

On the evening that He was betrayed, Jesus had a long discussion with His disciples in which He explained to them many important things. He told them about how He was going to prepare an eternal place for them, and of the promised Holy Spirit, and warned of the fiery hatred of the world. He did not promise them an easy life. In fact, He spoke to His disciples about the difficult path before them now. They would face much sorrow, and be persecuted by the world, and be put out of the synagogues. How would they make it through? One thing that Jesus revealed to them is the secret of the true vine. It would be the true vine that would guarantee fruitfulness in them, even in the midst of tribulation, and so prove them to be Christ's disciples.

Jesus taught His disciples, saying "I am the true vine" (John 15:1), and then explained its meaning. Before we shall proceed in examining this passage, however, we must stop and ask ourselves: What exactly did Jesus mean when He claimed to be the *true* vine? Or, put another way, how does the true vine differ from other vines?

The vine was a symbol that would have been ripe with meaning to any Jew in the days of Christ. While we might not pick up on the imagery Jesus was using here, the disciples would have understood immediately what He was referring to. Any Israelite present who was versed in the Old Testament scriptures would have been familiar with the typology of the vine, for it had long been in the Jewish religious teachings. The vine was a symbol of Israel's national life. It would be the same as if I gave a speech upon the steps of the capitol building and alluded to "the land of the free." Any American would immediately know I was talking about the United States. The same is true of the vine for the nation of Israel. The Old Testament prophets had long spoken of Israel as a vine:

> You brought a vine out of Egypt; you drove out the nations and planted it. (Psalm 80:8)

> And now, O inhabitants of Jerusalem and men of Judah, judge between me and my vineyard. What more was there to do for my vineyard, that I have not done in it? When I looked for it to yield grapes, why

did it yield wild grapes? (Isaiah 5:3-4)

Yet I planted you a choice vine, wholly a pure seed. How then have you turned degenerate and become a wild vine? (Jeremiah 2:21)

The prophets of old frequently used the symbol of the vine to typify that disappointing fruit the Israelites produced. Israel was a vine, but its fruit was evil. The nation only brought forth "wild grapes" that were worthless to God. The Lord's chosen people failed in bearing good fruit under the Old Covenant law. And we understand that this was really the purpose of the law. The law was given to reveal sin and to lead men to Jesus Christ (Galatians 3:24). The perfect law of God exposed Israel's sins—to prove them to be wicked and fruitless vines—that they might cry out to Him for mercy, forgiveness, and inner healing. Yet Israel did *none* of this, and instead kept producing wild grapes. They failed to fulfill their role in the covenant they swore at Sinai. So when Jesus stood amongst His disciples and told them that He was the true vine, He was acting as Israel's representative in fulfilling the Old Covenant law. Jesus Christ perfectly loved the Father, and kept the commandments, and had a perfect righteousness before God.

However, there is another sense in which Christ is the *true* vine. It is drawn from Jesus' comparison to other *physical* vines—the very ones that grow every year in vineyards for wine and produce. It is likely that Jesus may have held one of these gnarled little vines in His hands as He taught His disciples this mystery. When Jesus proclaimed that He is the *true* vine, it does not mean that other vines are false. He is not saying that other physical vines are not real vines. Instead, it means that throughout all eternity Jesus Christ has existed in relation to all things *as a vine. Jesus Christ is the real vine, the true.* He is the spiritual reality of which all other physical vines speak. And God created vines to give us a picture of what Jesus is to us. For Christ is the means of creation and sustainer of all reality:

> He is the image of the invisible God, the firstborn of all creation. For by him all things were created, in heaven and on earth, visible and invisible, whether thrones or dominions or rulers or authorities—all things were created through him and for him. And he is before all things, and in him all things hold together. (Colossians 1:15-17)

Everything that has ever been created, in heaven and on earth, whether it is massive supernovas or miniscule subatomic particles, everything was created by Jesus and through Jesus and for Jesus. All things and all people everywhere and at all times were created for Him and find their ultimate fulfillment and meaning in Jesus Christ. And this thought certainly includes vines. Jesus is the true vine, all other vines only whisper of His greatness. So we see that Christ is the ultimate reality behind all things.

The concept that Christ is the real spiritual substance and reality of things is not only true for vines. This is a consistent idea throughout the Scriptures. For example,

Jesus Christ is the *true* light that enlightens every man: "The true light, which enlightens everyone, was coming into the world. He was in the world, and the world was made through him, yet the world did not know him" (John 1:9-10). Likewise, Jesus is the *true* bread from heaven:

> Jesus then said to them, "Truly, truly, I say to you, it was not Moses who gave you bread from heaven, but my Father gives you the true bread from heaven. For the bread of God is he who comes down from heaven and gives life to the world." They said to him, "Sir, give us this bread always." (John 6:32-34)

The manna that God gave the Israelites in the wilderness was the shadow. The true bread from heaven, Jesus Christ, is the reality. In the same manner, the feasts and sacrificial law instituted at Sinai were all types and shadows of Christ (Colossians 2:16-17). The more I learn about the Bible, the more I understand it is all about Jesus. Everything in Scripture, in one way or another, points to Christ, whether it is a prophetic promise, a type or shadow, or a historical narrative weaving its way through history to the moment the eternal Word would be made flesh. Jesus Christ is all in all.

The vital reason that we need to know that Jesus is the true vine, which physical vines only point to, is this: Before there can be any talk of each of us being a branch, or bearing fruit, or the Father as the vinedresser, we need the Holy Spirit to illuminate to us the truth of Jesus Christ. Jesus *is* a vine. He will be to us *everything* that a vine is.

Christ will fill our lives with His life, He will nourish us and cause us to grow, and He will bear good fruit in our lives. Jesus Christ is the true vine, the real vine. Are you convinced of Him?

The Vinedresser

It is only in the context of Christ being the true vine that we can fully appreciate the Father's work as Vinedresser: "I am the true vine, and my Father is the vinedresser" (John 15:1). And we should first understand the eternal goal of the Father, as He moves us from branches that do "not bear fruit" (John 15:2), to branches that bear "fruit" (15:2), followed by "more fruit" (15:3), and finally to branches that bear "much fruit" (John 15:8). It is the mighty purpose of the New Covenant that every Christian becomes a branch that bears *much fruit*. The chief end of man is to glorify God and enjoy Him forever. And one way we do this is by bearing much fruit: "By this my Father is glorified, that you bear much fruit and so prove to be my disciples" (John 15:8).

The fruit brought forth in each of us brings glory to God and pleases the Vinedresser. And yet this is a process. No Christian begins their life in Jesus as a branch that bears much fruit. In fact, the progression of Christ's teaching here is analogous to the growth of every Christian. Before one repents and believes in Him it is impossible to bear *any* spiritual fruit. Those who are in the flesh cannot please God (Romans 8:8). It does not matter if one tries to do good, be charitable, or even have religious seal, for "without faith it is impossible to please him" (Hebrews 11:6). Apart from Jesus Christ and His righteousness we cannot please God. It is only *after* Christ has redeemed us that the Spirit can then bear fruit in us. As we grow and our awareness increases of our dependence upon Jesus, more fruit is formed in us. And so it is the Father's goal that every Christian becomes a branch that bears much fruit, to the glory of God.

The Father deals with each branch according to its need. Not all branches will receive the same treatment. As the expert Vinedresser, the Father's treatment depends on what is the nature of the vine He deems each to be: Certain branches He will take away. Other branches He prunes. And yet others, He lifts up. Let us explore the Father's work in His vineyard.

Christ explained what the Father does with each branch that does not bear fruit: "Every branch of mine that does not bear fruit he takes away... If anyone does not abide in me he is thrown away like a branch and withers; and the branches are gathered, thrown into the fire, and burned" (John 15:2,6). Every church has branches of this nature—little sucker shoots that latch on, yet remain fruitless. They can easily suck the life out of any church. Just what exactly *are* these branches? These are false converts, the goats who flock with Christ's sheep. The Scriptures explain the appearance of these people:

> Children, it is the last hour, and as you have heard that antichrist is coming, so now many antichrists have come. Therefore we know that it is the last hour. They went out from us, but they were not of us; for if they had been of us, they

> would have continued with us. But they
> went out, that it might become plain that
> they are not of us. (1 John 2:18-19)

There are those amongst us who are not *of* us, and many
will fall away, because they were *never* of us. And it is not
our duty to divide the sheep from the goats. We are not to
try to purge the fruitless branches from the vine. That is
the heavenly Vinedresser's work alone. Now, I'm not
undermining the importance of church discipline. Every
Biblical church should practice the guidelines for discipline
outlined in the New Testament. But as a general principle,
God will divide the wheat from the tares (Matthew 13:24-
30). The biggest reason that we shouldn't try to remove
what we think to be fruitless branches is the fact that we
cannot read another man's heart—often we do not even
know our own hearts! Consequently, all Christians are
called to examine themselves:

> Examine yourselves, to see whether you
> are in the faith. Test yourselves. Or do
> you not realize this about yourselves, that
> Jesus Christ is in you?—unless indeed you
> fail to meet the test! I hope that you will
> find out that we have not failed the test.
> (2 Corinthians 13:5-6)

What about the branches that *do* bear fruit? How
does the Father interact with them? He prunes! "Every
branch that does bear fruit he prunes, that it may bear
more fruit" (John15:2). The Lord prunes branches in
order that they might bear even more fruit. While the

Vinedresser prunes branches in many ways, two important methods of pruning come to mind as I am writing this.

The first picture of pruning is that of *brokenness*. While it is unpleasant for a branch to be pruned, it is often *more* painful for us to learn brokenness and dependence upon Jesus. Yet this process is necessary to fruitfulness. Consider the jars of clay in 2 Corinthians. The apostle Paul writes very passionately, that as jars of clay we contain an extraordinary treasure—the very life of Jesus Christ. And immediately what follows is this explanation:

> We are afflicted in every way, but not crushed; perplexed, but not driven to despair; persecuted, but not forsaken; struck down, but not destroyed; always carrying in the body the death of Jesus, so that the life of Jesus may also be manifested in our bodies. For we who live are always being given over to death for Jesus' sake, so that the life of Jesus also may be manifested in our mortal flesh. (2 Corinthians 4:8-11)

As a branch must be continually pruned to bear more fruit, the Christian must be continually given over to death— brokenness!—that Jesus Christ might be manifest. This process is painful, and it opens our deepest wounds to Him, but it really should cause us to rejoice because we know the glorious outcome: Spiritual fruitfulness, maturity, Jesus Christ, everything. I love Paul's explanation of the process and our proper response to it:

> So we do not lose heart. Though our
> outer nature is wasting away, our inner
> nature is being renewed day by day. For
> this slight momentary affliction is
> preparing for us an eternal weight of glory
> beyond all comprehension, as we look not
> to the things that are seen but to the
> things that are unseen. For the things
> that are seen are transient, but the things
> that are unseen are eternal. (2 Corinthians
> 4:16-18)

Are you looking to the things you see? Or are you looking to the eternal? While you suffer and feel the pain of brokenness, Jesus is there, He is with you and in you, and His fruit will grow on branches through even this. We must learn dependence upon Him. "For we were so utterly burdened beyond our strength that we despaired of life itself. Indeed, we felt that we had received the sentence of death. *But that was to make us rely not on ourselves but on God who raises the dead*" (2 Corinthians 1:8-9).

Certainly the Father desires brokenness in our innermost being. David wrote, "The sacrifices of God are a broken spirit; a broken and contrite heart, O God, you will not despise" (Psalm 51:17). And while it is natural for branches to depend on the life of the vine in order to bear fruit, many Christians naturally try to do the opposite. They try to form life in themselves and bear fruit for God. This is dead works. This is why brokenness is so powerful. We must accept the affliction, the death, the pruning, and look to the eternal. We must learn to be continually weak, in order to prove that all of our strength is found only in Jesus. "For when I am weak, then I am strong" (2 Corinthians 12:10).

The second picture of pruning comes from the Father's discipline. Very often, Christians will hold onto sinful desires and habits for a long time, and this will rob us of many opportunities to bear good fruit. So God prunes us, He disciplines us. And this is a *good* thing. He will not allow any of His children to wallow in wickedness and filth, but will discipline us to set us on a path that is both good for us and glorifying to Him:

> It is for discipline that you have to endure. God is treating you as sons. For what son is there whom his father does not discipline? If you are left without discipline, in which you all have participated, then you are illegitimate children and not sons. (Hebrews 12:7-8)

If we are allowed to sin, and to remain in our sins, then we are illegitimate sons and not *really* children of God. God firmly and lovingly deals with each of us when we are caught in sin, leading us to repentance and a restored fellowship with Him. He deals with us not only as the Vinedresser, but as our heavenly Father who loves us very much. He is involved in the details. He is the one by which we cry out, "Abba! Father!" (Romans 8:15). His love is much too immense to allow His children to have anything less than to yield the fruit of righteousness—that which is *also* glorifying to Him. "By this my Father is glorified, that you bear much fruit and so prove to be my disciples" (John 15:8). He disciplines us as a loving Father:

> Besides this, we have had earthly fathers who disciplined us and we respected them. Shall we not much more be subject to the Father of spirits and live? For they disciplined us for a short time as it seemed best to them, but *he disciplines us for our good, that we may share his holiness.* For the moment all discipline seems painful rather than pleasant, but later it yields the peaceful fruit of righteousness to those who have been trained by it. (Hebrews 12:9-11)

God disciplines us for our own good, that we may have lives of true righteousness and holiness. The heavenly Father is working to make us holy (whole) people, remember? And while this process of pruning can be painful, the Vinedresser must prune branches to keep them fruitful. Anything less would prove God to not be a loving Father.

ABIDING IN JESUS CHRIST

Finally, we come to abiding. There are a few conditions that must be met in order for a Christian to abide in Christ. First of all, we need to have had a cleansing—our justification. This can be seen when Christ explains, "Already you are clean because of the word that I have spoken to you" (John 15:3). It is only those who have been justified—all who have responded to the Gospel by repenting of their sins and trusting in Jesus

Christ—who have begun their life in Christ and thus can abide in Him. When we were justified not only did the blood of the Lamb cleanse us from all unrighteousness, but we have also been placed into Jesus Christ. He is now our righteousness, our sanctification, our life, our wisdom, our everything. "He is the source of your life in Christ Jesus, whom God made our wisdom and our righteousness and sanctification and redemption" (1 Corinthians 1:30). I can think of no clearer meaning of Christ being the True Vine and we His branches than that Christ *is* our life and righteousness and everything. Jesus Christ is the vine, the stem, the leaves, the fruit—He is our all in all. And so just as a branch must be grafted into a vine in order for it to have the vine's life flowing through it, so must a man be placed into Christ.

The second condition that must be met is that we must actually *abide*. "Abide in me, and I in you. As a branch cannot bear fruit by itself, unless it abides in the vine, neither can you, unless you abide in me" (John 15:4). While the branches' cleansing is our justification, the branches' abiding is our *sanctification*. Every branch must abide in Him for fruit—Jesus declared, "Whoever abides in me and I in him, he it is that bears much fruit, for apart from me you can do nothing" (John 15:5). Sadly, many Christians try to bear fruit *for* God apart from Jesus, yet this is the one thing they cannot do! Sincerity does not matter in bearing fruit, nor observance of the law, apart from the True Vine all will fail. *When Christ taught, "Unless you abide in me," it means that there is no other way for us to bear fruit than by Him.*

I do not understand why this truth is not shared more frequently from the pulpit. Pastors and teachers can throw all the three-point sermons, books, spiritual formulas, and the like at congregations, but it will do them no good—will bear no fruit—unless it is prefaced with the words, "Unless you abide in Jesus Christ."

Now, "abiding" clearly does not mean the same thing as merely being "in Christ." All Christians are in Christ, yet not all practice abiding in Him. While being "in Christ" is a matter of position and identity, "abiding" is a matter of practice. *Abiding in Christ is a matter of deliberate, consistent and conscious communion with Jesus.* When we realize we are unable to do anything, and instead look away to Jesus to be our sufficiency in all things, we are abiding in Him. So then abiding speaks of dependence and fruitfulness.

When Jesus Christ spoke to His disciples, "Abide in me, and I in you" (John 15:4), this was given as a command. Abiding is therefore a thing that Christians *must* learn to practice. It comes with a condition of responsibility. We must respond to Christ's call to abide! It is something that we must do; and within it is contained both a note of activity and one of passivity. There is a responsibility we must live by in faith (activity) and a work that we must done within us (passivity). Let us examine both.

Christ's command to abide in Him is a command to activity. When Jesus says, "Abide in me," there is a vital choice to be made: Will we choose things that expose ourselves to Him? Will we take hold of the means of grace that the Lord has given us to encounter and know Christ? I am speaking of such things as exposing ourselves to the Bible, prayer, fellowship with other believers, the sacraments, worship—these are all tangible means to know

Jesus Christ. This idea is further illuminated by the words that Christ later spoke, "If you abide in me, and my words abide in you, ask whatever you wish, and it will be done for you" (John 15:7). Here are mentioned what are probably the two most important activities young branches can partake, the ones in which our faith is most built up and purely expressed: The Word and prayer. Having Christ's words abide in us and then asking whatever we wish—these together are the first task for Christians; these are how branches can abide in the True Vine.

Likewise, Jesus wants to abide in us: "Abide in me, and *I in you*" (John 15:4). He is speaking to our hearts: "Let Me abide in you." This too is a command, but it is given with a slightly difference nuance. As we have learned, the life of Christ dwells within us, imparted to us though our unity with Jesus in His resurrection. Now He wants this same life to abide in us. While this is given as a command, it is not a command to *do* anything. Jesus' desire for His life to abide in us is not a command to activity. Instead, this is a command of *passivity* and comes with yet another choice to be made: Will we allow His life to be expressed within us? Will we allow the person of Jesus Christ to be our sufficiency in all things? This crucial decision is essential for a fruitful life, for Christ proclaimed, "I am the vine; you are the branches. Whoever abides in me and I in him, he it is that bears much fruit, for apart from me you can do nothing" (John 15:5). We cannot bear fruit by ourselves, we cannot do *anything* apart from the life of Jesus Christ—we *must* have Him abiding in us.

A further explanation of what abiding is like comes from the time that Jesus explained that He was the True

Bread from heaven, of which the manna in the wilderness was only a shadow. The manna provided the Israelites nourishment and sustained them for some time, yet eventually all who had eaten the manna died. Christ—as the Bread of Life—was not so. If anyone ate of Him, they would live forever. "I am the living bread that came down from heaven. If anyone eats of this bread, he will live forever. And the bread that I will give for the life of the world is my flesh" (John 6:51). This statement troubled the Jews. They groaned to Jesus and did not understand how anyone could eat His flesh. Yet Christ explained further, and in this statement we find what our abiding should be:

> So Jesus said to them, "Truly, truly, I say to you, unless you eat the flesh of the Son of Man and drink his blood, you have no life in you. Whoever feeds on my flesh and drinks my blood has eternal life, and I will raise him up on the last day. For my flesh is true food, and my blood is true drink. *Whoever feeds on my flesh and drinks my blood abides in me, and I in him.* As the living Father sent me, and I live because of the Father, so whoever feeds on me, he also will live because of me. This is the bread that came down from heaven, not as the fathers ate and died. Whoever feeds on this bread will live forever." (John 6:53-58)

Will you eat of His flesh and drink of His blood? *His life abiding in us should be more important than the food we eat.* We must be so fixated on the person of Jesus Christ that our hearts are consumed by Him. We must be so convinced of our dependence upon Him that it is as if we are eating His flesh and drinking His blood. This dependence is as intimate as the food we eat and the things we drink. This should be our single heartbeat, our prayer, our song. This is what abiding should look like.

Christ wants His life to abide in us. This is our single source of enablement and empowerment. If we abide in Him, and He in us, we will bear much fruit. If we do not allow Him to abide in us, we will bear *no* fruit whatsoever. The difference between abiding and not abiding is the difference between night and day, between being a good tree and a bad one. The kind of fruit that we produce will naturally follow what kind of tree we are. Jesus once spoke:

> "You will recognize them by their fruits. Are grapes gathered from thornbushes, or figs from thistles? So, every healthy tree bears good fruit, but the diseased tree bears bad fruit. A healthy tree cannot bear bad fruit, nor can a diseased tree bear good fruit. Every tree that does not bear good fruit is cut down and thrown into the fire. Thus you will recognize them by their fruits." (Matthew 7:16-20)

While Christ is specifically referring here to how we can recognize false prophets and teachers, the principle remains true: Good trees produce good fruit, and bad tree

produce bad fruit. And what exactly *is* the fruit that we—
if we abide in Jesus and thus are good vines—will bear? It
is none other than the fruit of the Holy Spirit:

> But the fruit of the Spirit is love, joy,
> peace, patience, kindness, goodness,
> faithfulness, gentleness, self-control;
> against such things there is no law.
> (Galatians 5:22-23)

Here Christ is being formed in each of us. He is bearing
good fruit through the ministry of the Holy Spirit. It
should instantly come to our minds that this is the
fulfillment of a New Covenant promise: "And I will put
my Spirit within you, and cause you to walk in my statutes
and be careful to obey my rules" (Ezekiel 36:27). The
Spirit of God is being breathed into you, He is sweeping
through your life as a mighty wind, mediating Christ's
presence to you, making manifest His life in your mortal
body. One thing that I love about the idea of abiding in
Christ is how it comes hand-in-hand with obedience. This
is the consistent message throughout Scripture:

> And by this we know that we have come
> to know him, if we keep his
> commandments. Whoever says "I know
> him" but does not keep his
> commandments is a liar, and the truth is
> not in him, but whoever keeps his word,
> in him truly the love of God is perfected.
> By this we may be sure that we are in him:
> Whoever says he abide in him ought to

walk in the same way in which he walked.
(1 John 2:3-6)

The apostle John goes on to write, "Whoever keeps his commandments abides in him, and he in them. And by this we know that he abides in us, by the Spirit whom he has given us" (1 John 3:24). So we see that everything forms together beautifully: The person and character of Jesus Christ being formed in us, the ministry of the Holy Spirit and obedience to the Law of God as a result; all come by abiding in Jesus. As frail branches we must learn to trust and abide in Jesus Christ, for all our fruitfulness and power is found in Him.

CHAPTER 10 – THE SECRET OF THE YOKE OF JESUS

So then, there remains a Sabbath rest for the
people of God, for whoever has entered God's rest
has also rested from his works as God did from
his. (Hebrews 4:9-10)

SEATED WITH CHRIST

We are told in the book of Ephesians that the Father (after the Christ had been crucified) "raised him from the dead and seated him at his right hand in the heavenly places" (Ephesians 1:20). After His resurrection and ascension, Jesus *sat down* at the right hand of the Father. In the same way, those of us who are in Jesus Christ are told that God "raised us up with him and seated us with him in the heavenly places in Christ" (Ephesians 2:6). Our position of being seated with Him is by virtue of our identity in Christ ("seated us with Him… *in Christ*"). Every spiritual blessing a Christian has comes by way of being in Christ. The apostle Paul opens his epistle by reminding the Ephesians that the Father has "blessed us in Christ with every spiritual blessing" (Ephesians 1:3). And this certainly includes our position of being seated with Jesus Christ at the right hand of the Almighty.

All of this has immense significance. First of all, through our unity with Jesus in His resurrection, we have been born again to new spiritual life, and now there is a part of our being that functions in the heavenly domain, right now. At this very moment, if you are in Christ, you are seated with Him in the heavenly places. We *must* understand this. *In this very moment we are now seated with Jesus in the heavenly places.* However, that is not to say that heaven isn't a place that we will go when we die. It certainly *includes* that, but heaven is also more than just that:

> For we know that if the tent, which is our earthly home, is destroyed, we have a building from God, a house not made with hands, eternal in the heavens. For in this tent we groan, longing to put on our heavenly dwelling, if indeed by putting it on we may not be found naked. For while we are still in this tent, we groan, being burdened—not that we would be unclothed, but *that we would be further clothed*, so that what is mortal may be swallowed up by life. He who has prepared us for this very thing is God, who has given us the Spirit as a guarantee. (2 Corinthians 5:1-5)

The tent mentioned here echoes the tabernacle (the true one in heaven), which we have already discussed. But the idea here is that we shall be "*further* clothed," meaning that part of our being is operating in the spiritual domain right now, and the fullness of this heavenly reality will come only after death. Yes, part of ourselves are seated with Christ in the heavenly places now, but one day our resurrection bodies will walk in the New Jerusalem. We will meet at the tree of life, my dear, and eat of its twelve kinds of fruit.

Another point that must be made is to note that our Heavenly Father has "*seated* us with him in the heavenly places in Christ" (Ephesians 2:6). Just as Jesus has *already* sat down at the right hand of the Father, we must see that, as Christians, we likewise have *already* been seated. Sitting is a position of rest. There is no need for us to try and sit down, but instead the Spirit of God must illuminate to us that we have already have been seated. Jesus has been seated and we are today seated with Him.

Putting everything together—our mystical union with Jesus, our current functioning in the heavenly places, and our position of being seated with Christ; we must understand one thing: *Our strength as Christians comes only from a position of rest.* Jesus Christ died for our sins, was buried, raised on the third day, and is exalted and seated at the right hand of the Father. There is nothing more needed to be added from ourselves. Our rest first comes from Christ's rest, for He is seated because His work is complete—"It is finished!" (John 19:30). This is also clear in Hebrews: "After making purification for sins, he *sat down* at the right hand of the Majesty on high" (Hebrews 1:3). Thus, after the resurrection, Jesus took a position of *rest.* In the same manner, our strength comes from resting in Christ's finished work, along with resting in His indwelling life for our sanctification. Now we must ask ourselves this vital question: How are we to find rest for our souls in Him?

A PROMISE OF REST

It is of vital importance that every believer in Jesus Christ enters into God's rest. The author of Hebrews spends nearly two chapters laboring this crucial idea (Hebrews 3-4). The writer gives a sober warning that we should take great care not fail to reach this rest. "Therefore, while the promise of entering his rest still stands, let us fear lest any of you should seem to have failed to reach it" (Hebrews 4:1). Failing to find the rest of God is something that many Christians apparently do. They strive and work, but never find rest for their souls in Jesus Christ. Jesus called out, "Come to me, all who labor and are heavy laden, and I will give you rest. Take my yoke upon you and learn from me, for I am gently and lowly in heart, and you will find rest for your souls" (Matthew 11:28-29). Would you like to learn the secret of the easy yoke? Let us explore just what God's rest looks like and how we are to enter into it. Jesus' yoke is easy, His burden is light.

We are told that a great rest is available to the people of God. Two examples are given to us to show what this rest looks like. First, the rest is likened to the nation of Israel entering into the Promised Land (Hebrews 3:7-19). The land that was promised to Abraham would provide *rest* for the wandering Israelites. This is given as an allegory for the Christian's rest in Christ. The other example of rest is a picture of Sabbath rest (Hebrews 4:3-10). Consequently, the rest we experience may be understood by remembering that God rested from all His works on the seventh day of creation. "For he has somewhere spoken of the seventh day in this way: 'And God rested on the seventh day from all his works...' So then, there remains a Sabbath rest for the people of God" (Hebrews 4:4, 10). Let's look at both of these examples.

THE REST OF THE PROMISED LAND

The rest of God is likened to the Israelites entering the Promised Land. After wandering for forty years and dying in the desert heat, the children of Jacob were allowed to enter the rest of the Promised Land and find relief. How are we to find this rest? The apostle Paul gives us a brief synopsis of the Exodus account in his letter to the Corinthians. He tells us that these things were written down for our instruction, in order that we may learn from the Israelites' mistakes. Since every believer is called to make an exodus of their own into God's rest—our promised land—it would benefit us to consider the Israelite's journey:

> I want you to know brothers, that our fathers were all under the cloud, and all passed through the sea, and all were baptized into Moses in the cloud and in the sea, and all ate the same spiritual food,

> and all drank the same spiritual drink.
> For they drank from the spiritual Rock
> that followed them, and the Rock was
> Christ. Nevertheless, with most of them
> God was not pleased, for they were
> overthrown in the wilderness. (1
> Corinthians 10:1-5)

Even though they all drank from the spiritual rock, which is Jesus Christ, nevertheless the Lord was displeased with them. While they certainly received many blessings, signs, and miracles, yet even all of these were not enough and they went astray. They were deceived by evil. In the end, what happened to them? They were not allowed to enter into the rest of the land promised to Abraham! And so the died in the wilderness:

> Now these things took place as examples
> to us, that we might not desire evil as they
> did. Do not be idolaters as some of them
> were; as it is written, "The people sat
> down to eat and drink and rose up to
> play." We must not indulge in sexual
> immorality as some of them did, and
> twenty-three thousand fell in a single day.
> We must not put Christ to the test, as
> some of them did and were destroyed by
> serpents, nor grumble, as some of them
> did and were destroyed by the Destroyer.
> (1 Corinthians 10:6-10)

The Israelites committed idolatry, sexual immorality, and

tested the Lord, just to highlight some of their wickedness. What was really happening? *Their hearts were hardened by the deceitfulness of sin.* They had become the harlot of Jacob and it cost them dearly. Spiritual unfaithfulness is not a trivial thing. Although God was patient and longsuffering towards His people, their wickedness was far too extensive. They never remained faithful to the Lord. Through their continual disobedience their hearts became calloused and cold towards the things of God. And this very same thing can happen to us. Sin can creep into our lives and deceive us, and we can lose desire for the Lord. This is the warning given in Hebrews:

> Take care, brothers, lest there be in any of
> you an evil, unbelieving heart, leading you
> to fall away from the living God. But
> exhort one another every day, as long as it
> is called "today," that none of you may be
> hardened by the deceitfulness of sin. For
> we share in Christ, if indeed we hold our
> original confidence firm to the end.
> (Hebrews 3:12-14)

Israel's disobedience ultimately led God to swear in His wrath that they would not enter into His rest. An entire generation was not allowed to set a single foot into the land promised to Abraham, but instead died in the desolate places. *And these things are given to us as a warning, lest we should desire evil as they did.* We have been given a great number of blessings in Jesus Christ, yet God desires faithfulness in our inner being: "For we share in Christ, if indeed we hold our original confidence firm to the end"

(Hebrews 3:14).   The Israelites were granted mighty blessings by the Lord, just as we are now. We would do well to learn from their mistakes! We must not indulge in immorality, but rather be faithful to what the Lord has called us. The deceitfulness of sin is one way we will fall short of reaching God's perfect rest.

SABBATH REST

However, the Israelites did not wander in the wilderness forever. Eventually the day came when a new leader, Joshua, led them on a conquest into the Promised Land. They received the rest that their fathers should have entered.   And yet the writer of Hebrews makes a vital point: There is "another day" of rest, written about years later in the Psalms through King David:

> Since therefore it remains for some to enter it, and those who formerly received the good news failed to enter because of disobedience, again he appoints a certain day, "Today," saying though David so long afterward, in the words already quoted, "Today, if you hear his voice, do not harden your hearts." For if Joshua had given them rest, God would not have spoken of *another* day later on. (Hebrews 4:6-8)

This passage quoted in Hebrews is taken from Psalm 95:7-11.   It is important to note that although the psalm is clearly discussing Israel's rebellion in the wilderness, the author of Hebrews speaks of another day, "Today," where there is a call to not turn a blind eye and fail to enter the rest of God. This rest, instead of being likened to the rest of the Promised Land, is pictured as a Sabbath rest. "So then, there remains a Sabbath rest for the people of God, for whoever has entered God's rest has also rested from his works as God did from his" (Hebrews 4:9-10).

There remains a Sabbath rest for the people of God, who rest from their works as He did after creation. *This is a spiritual rest.* The physical Sabbath rest was only a shadow of a deeper heavenly reality. The Almighty instructed His people on Mount Sinai, telling them, "Remember the Sabbath day, to keep it holy" (Exodus 20:8). And keeping the Sabbath holy was a shadow of the true rest God has for His people. The substance of Sabbath rest is ultimately found in Jesus Christ:

> Therefore let no one pass judgment on you in questions of food and drink, or with regard to a festival or a new moon or a Sabbath. These are a shadow of the things to come, but the substance belongs to Christ. (Colossians 2:16-17)

In many things there is found a heavenly reality, one that is just as real—no, *more* real—than the shadow or physical reality. In vines we see the True Vine, which is Christ (John 15:1). We discover that the ancient tabernacle is a mere copy of the true in heaven (Hebrews 8:5). And in Sabbath rest we find the true rest that Jesus Christ gives to a child of God. The writer of Hebrews is explaining

Sabbath rest *not* as simply a day of the week. If that were the case, he would have spoken of *many* Sabbath rests remaining for the people of God, instead of *a* Sabbath rest. *The Sabbath rest available to those in Christ is none other than Jesus Christ.* Those who rest from their works as God did His, and trust in Jesus' death and resurrection, as well as His Spirit inside of them are experiencing Sabbath rest. Those trusting in the works of the flesh are not. Jesus will to express His life through those He redeemed and will give them rest. When Christ is allowed to be our sufficiency in any area of our life, then we are experiencing true Sabbath rest. So there *remains* a Sabbath rest for the people of God.

After explaining Sabbath rest, the author of Hebrews presents us with a challenge that may seem—at least at first—a bit out of place:

> Let us therefore strive to enter that rest, so that no one may fall by the same sort of disobedience. For the word of God is living and active, sharper than any two-edged sword, piercing to the division of soul and spirit, of joints and marrow, and discerning the thoughts and intentions of the heart. And no creature is hidden from his sight, but all are naked and exposed to the eyes of him to whom we must give account. (Hebrews 4:11-13)

If we pause and consider how often we scarcely know our own hearts and motives, and the need to daily examine ourselves, these verses make perfect sense. They fit seamlessly into the train of thought here. As each of us make our great exodus journey and learn trust and intimacy with Jesus, we must always allow the Word of God to constantly judge us, to sift our hearts and motives, to keep us resting in Christ. This is the way to maturity and true spirituality. If we neglect the Scriptures, our lives can quickly turn into a mess. The Word of God will cut each one of us like a mighty sword of the Holy Spirit, leaving barren the thoughts and intentions of our hearts, in order that we may press on towards the upward calling of Jesus Christ. Let us strive to find our rest in Him.

WALKING BY FAITH

The entire passage about Sabbath rest is given as a warning. The author of Hebrews urges us not to miss out on entering God's rest. It is a thing that many Christians fail to reach. And there is one paragraph on this matter that is particularly illuminating:

> Therefore, while the promise of entering his rest still stands, let us fear lest any of you should seem to have failed to reach it. For good news came to us just as to them, but the message they heard did not benefit them, because they were not united by faith with those who listened. (Hebrews 4:1-2)

It is here that we find the great secret of entering God's rest. Conversely, it is these verses that reveal the wickedest sin, the ultimate tragedy, the one thing that *guarantees* a

Christian will not enter rest. It is the absence of faith. We indeed read some good news here in Hebrews— hallelujah!—and yet must not fail to grasp this critical point. *The reason that the message the Israelites heard did not benefit them was because it was not accepted by faith.* Likewise, the ultimate reason a Christian may fail to enter the Lord's rest is because they do not hear the word by faith. And unbelief is a grave sin: "For whatever does not proceed from faith is sin" (Romans 14:23).

We must be careful to take the truths in the Bible and unite them with faith. If we do not do this, we will fail to see the reality of God's truth made manifest in our lives. As I search the Scriptures, I'm discovering that the idea of "walking by faith" (2 Corinthians 5:7) is *profound.* This depth is due to the immense practicality of taking the things we read in the Scriptures and uniting them with faith. The Spirit of God illuminates truth to each of us in the Bible, but if we fail to act upon it, the truth will do us no good. Truth not acted upon will ultimately be lost. And so we must walk by faith.

Faith always stands upon God's truth. Not only is faith the acceptance of God's fact, it is the vehicle by which truth is appropriated in a Christian's life. Faith is a *response* to what God has promised. It is an active trust in what the Lord has declared to be true. All truth in the Bible does us almost no good unless it is acted upon. For example, the gospel does little good if it falls upon deaf ears. One must respond to the gospel by confessing with their mouth, "Jesus is Lord," and believing in their heart that He rose from the dead in order to be saved (Romans 10:10). That is the acceptance of faith. And yet if the gospel isn't responded to by faith, it will only serve as further condemnation at the final judgment. This is only one example. The Lord gives divine truth all the time. Each time the Spirit illuminates Biblical truth to us we *must* respond to it. We must unite it with faith. The dismal reality is that truth not acted upon is ultimately lost.

And yet one thing should be added here. *Faith itself comes by the word of Christ.* "So faith comes by hearing, and hearing through the word of Christ" (Romans 10:17). Whenever Christ is preached faith is created. Every Christian must continually here the gospel and be exposed to what Jesus Christ has done and who He is, for faith then comes and we rest in Jesus. This is our Sabbath rest, our Promised Land, it is trusting in Christ and His death, burial, and resurrection.

Here is a critical point that James, the brother of Jesus, makes in his letter to the twelve tribes. He explains an important distinction that faith without works is dead:

> What good is it, my brothers, if someone says he has faith but does not have works? Can that faith save him? If a brother or sister is poorly clothed and lacking in daily food, and one of you says to them, "Go in peace, be warmed and filled," without giving them the things needed for his body, what good is that? So also faith by itself, if it does not have works, is dead. (James 2:14-17)

Here James makes a point, by way of example, that if a person wishes the poor and destitute to be well and yet doesn't *actually* help them, that person's faith is not genuine. It is nonexistent. Only the person who actually helps the poor in practice has real faith. James goes on:

> But someone will say, "You have faith and I have works." Show me your faith apart from your works, and I will show you my faith by my works. You believe that God is one; you do well. Even the demons believe—and shudder! (James 2:18-19)

James underscores in these verses that faith is not merely an agreement to truth, because even the demons know the truth. They know what the truth is alright, although they pervert the truth with lies. Finally, James gives us the example of the story of Abraham, who "believed the Lord and he counted it to him as righteousness" (Genesis 15:6). Abraham's story is the primary illustration of faith at work:

> Do you want to be shown, you foolish person, that faith apart from works is useless? Was not Abraham our father justified by works when he offered up his son Isaac on the altar? You see that faith was active along with his works, and faith was completed by his works; and the Scripture was fulfilled that says, "Abraham believed God, and it was counted to him as righteousness"—and he was called a friend of God. (James 2:20-23)

Abraham's faith "was completed by his works" (James 2:22). That is the nature of faith. It is not only belief in what God has declared to be true, but a belief that puts itself into practice. Biblical faith is characterized by action and a heartfelt response to God's Word. Faith is not a passive thing. It is dynamic. I liken faith to chairs. You can know everything about chairs—the history or chairs, their construction, all the varieties and uses of chairs. You may even have a large selection of chairs at home. Perhaps some of them were given to you as gifts and so hold deep personal meaning and invoke an emotional response when you think of them. You may even believe that a certain chair will hold your weight if you chose to sit in it. Yet will this mere knowledge ever give you *rest*? Of course not! A man finds rest only when he sits in a chair. This is the difference between belief and faith. Those in Christ walk by faith when we apply and rest in what the Lord declares in Scripture. For example, we read that Jesus Christ is "our wisdom and our righteousness and sanctification and redemption" (1 Corinthians 1:30). The rest of faith causes us to cease to trust in our own righteousness and look to Jesus. Likewise, the rest of faith allows us to not trust in ourselves for sanctification, but to look to Christ for sanctification. The same is true of wisdom, and redemption, and everything. Jesus Christ warmly offers us rest for our souls!

We need only to look at an example in Hebrews to see if we grasp the essence of faith. Israel's failure to enter the Promised Land was due to their lack of faith. They did not take the things that they were told and unite them with faith. Now, let us turn this issue upon its head. Could the Israelites have possessed faith—real faith—and still *not* have entered into the Promised Land? No! That is not what Biblical faith consists of—"Show me your faith apart from your works, and I will show you my faith by my works…" (James 2:18). Faith, by its very nature, required the Israelites to enter into and possess the Promised Land. Certainly, this is what the prophet Habakkuk meant when the Lord spoke though him and said, "The righteous shall live by his faith" (Habakkuk 2:4). Faith of this quality will guard your heart like a shield, strong and true.

The clearest definition we have of faith is found in the book of Hebrews:

> Now faith is the assurance of things hoped for, the conviction of things not seen. For by it the people of old received their commendation. By faith we understand that the universe was created by the word of God, so that what is seen was not made out of things that are visible. (Hebrews 11:1-3)

The Holy Spirit builds me up when I read that faith consists of "the conviction of things not seen" (Hebrews 11:1). It illuminates what the apostle Paul meant when he wrote that "we walk by faith, not by sight" (2 Corinthians 5:7). As we grow in Jesus Christ, we cannot physically see God transforming our hearts and conforming each of us to the image of the Son. There is no scientific experiment that can be done, no litmus test to verify our sanctification empirically. We can only see the *result* of sanctification as the Spirit forms fruit in our lives. And although we can't see it with our eyes, yet we still walk. We press on. We walk by faith. Our Christian walk, however, is in "the assurance of things hoped for, the conviction of things not seen" (Hebrews 11:1). Oh, how I love to meditate upon the saints of old, with all the mighty works that the Lord did through them. In the middle of this chapter, however, we're left with these words on the requirement of faith: "And without faith it is impossible to please him, for whoever would draw near to God must believe that he exists and that he rewards those who seek him" (Hebrews 11:6). This is how we are to walk by faith, daily trusting that the Lord will do and complete the work He promised to do in each of us. We run the race set before us, always "looking to Jesus, the founder and perfecter of our faith" (Hebrews 12:2).

THE YOKE OF CHRIST

With our understanding of the essence of faith, we quickly discover that true Sabbath rest is not a rest *from* work, but a rest *in* work. Trusting in Jesus to be our sufficiency in all things does not lead to passivity and inactivity. In fact, it is the opposite—it leads to a radical life where we trust in and respond to the promises of God. A person who misunderstands Sabbath rest may believe that it will lead Christians to living passive lives, but this is an error. Sabbath rest is trusting in the Lord Jesus Christ to fulfill the promises in His word, especially the promises of the New Covenant. Consequently, as we walk and serve the Lord in the faithfulness, we must understand the necessity to cease from all forms of self-effort and instead to depend upon the indwelling life of Christ. We will find strength in the midst of weakness. We must hear the words of Christ:

> "Come to me, all who labor and are heavy laden, and I will give you rest. Take my yoke upon you, and learn from me, from I am gentle and lowly in heart, and you will find rest for your souls. For my yoke is easy, and my burden is light." (Matthew 11:28-30).

Will you come to Christ? He will give you rest for your soul. Here again is the crucial difference between the genuine rest of faith and every other sham perpetrated upon Christianity. What Christian receives the rest that Jesus declared? Is it the one who merely reads these words and believes them to be true? Of course not. It is the Christian who reads these words, knows them to be true, and responds to them in faith by actually coming to Christ, taking His yoke upon himself, and learning from Jesus. That is the man who receives rest. So Sabbath rest really is a rest in the midst of work and not a rest from it. The rest of faith—real rest; deep Sabbath rest and the rest of the Promised Land—still means that we continue to work. We are still plowing the field. The only difference is that *our* yoke is shared with Jesus and He does all the heavy pulling.

I would like to encourage you with one last thing. It is a call that the writer of Hebrews gives to us: "Let us therefore strive to enter that rest, so that no one may fall by the same sort of disobedience" (Hebrews 4:11). I am constantly amazed at the paradox of the need to *strive* for rest. But that is the charge we are given here. Yes, today if you hear the voice of the Lord in His Word, give up the self-effort, the constant struggles, the furiously empty business, and instead depend upon the mighty and constant life of Jesus Christ for your victory. His yoke is easy. His burden is light.

CHAPTER 11 – THE ARMOR OF GOD

Therefore take up the whole armor of God, that
you may be able to withstand the evil day, and
having done all, to stand firm. (Ephesians 6:13)

SPIRITUAL WARFARE

There is a war going on. It is invisible, it is all around us, and most of all it is *spiritual*. The enemy prowls around like a roaring lion, looking for someone to devour. Yes, there is a war going on, and *we* are in it. The war has been waged since the dawn of time, and although the battle certainly belongs to the Lord, we must not take our adversary lightly. If only we knew the forces that have set themselves against us! And if we desire to grow strong in our faith, it is vital that we understand spiritual warfare. We must discover what the Christian's role is in this cosmic battle.

When Jesus was in the synagogue in Nazareth, He read from the book of Isaiah:

> And he came to Nazareth, where he had been brought up. And as was his custom, he went to the synagogue on the Sabbath day, and he stood up to read. And the scroll of the prophet Isaiah was given to him. He unrolled the scroll and found the place where it was written, "The Spirit of the Lord is upon me, because he has anointed me to proclaim good news to the poor. He has sent me to proclaim liberty to the captives and recovering of sight to the blind, to set at liberty those who are oppressed, to proclaim the year of the Lord's favor." (Luke 4:16-19)

Christ read these words in the midst of the congregation. These were words of hope, words of freedom, and most importantly, these were words about Jesus. The hearts of all the people must have burned inside of them when they heard Christ read these words, because we read that every person's eyes were firmly fixed on Jesus. What He did next was magnificent:

> And he rolled up the scroll and gave it back to the attendant and sat down. And the eyes of all in the synagogue were fixed on him. And he began to say to them, "Today this Scripture has been fulfilled in your hearing." (Luke 4:20-21)

Jesus Christ came to free the captives, just as this prophecy foretold. What we might not perceive at first, however, is that the captivity described here is a *spiritual* one. Every lost person is a captive of Satan, and Jesus came to release captives from the devil's grasp. The spiritual battle being fought, therefore, is a war over the souls of mankind. We are caught in the middle of this battle; we are under our commander the Lord Jesus Christ. The devil seeks to keep the lost souls of this world captive and in darkness, while Christ came to bring freedom, light, and life.

We are given clear directions in the epistle to the Ephesians on how we are to participate in this cosmic battle and not be defeated by the schemes of our foe, Satan. The apostle Paul writes, "Finally, be strong in the Lord and in the strength of his might. Put on the whole armor of God, that you may be able to stand against the schemes of the devil" (Ephesians 6:10-11). As those in Christ, we must be strong in the Lord and in the strength of His might. This is the only way we can handle the struggle and fight the good fight. We are never told that the Christian life is meant to be easy. While Christ certainly promised abundant life to each of His sheep, He never said our time on this world would be comfortable. In fact, this passage would lead someone to believe quite otherwise. Even sheep with the best shepherd face dangers from lions and bears. The book of Ephesians lets us understand that one of the primary characteristics of the Christian life can be summed up in one word: Wrestle. As Christians we wrestle—we struggle—against the evil forces and cosmic powers of this veiled world. "For we do not *wrestle* against flesh and blood, but against the rulers, against the authorities, against the cosmic powers over this present darkness, against the spiritual forces of evil in the heavenly places" (Ephesians 6:12). While every man is opposed by these demonic forces, only Christians may wrestle *against* them. Every other person, regardless of religion, faith or creed, is a prisoner in this battle. And so it is of utmost importance that we learn to be strong in the Lord and the strength of His might. How are we to do this?

The apostle Paul elaborates on how we are to be strong in the Lord and the strength of His might. It is by putting on the full armor of God: "Therefore take up the whole armor of God, that you may be able to withstand in the evil day, and having done all, to stand firm" (Ephesians 6:13). As we shall see very soon, *the armor is profound.* If we would step into the armory and briefly meditate upon each piece of the armor of God, we would find that the weapons we possess are more than adequate to help us overcome and to stand in the evil day. It is written else ware in Scripture: "For though we walk in the flesh, we are not waging war according to the flesh. For the weapons of our warfare are not of the flesh but have divine power to destroy strongholds" (2 Corinthians 10:3-4). Our weapons are not of this world, but they are mighty, through the Lord, that we may take down any strongholds in our path and bring into captivity every thought to the obedience to Jesus Christ.

Before we can study each individual piece of the armor, we must come to terms with just what the armor is. The armor of God, instead of being merely a figure of speech or a metaphor, is actually the symbol of something *real.* Like so many of the topics we have previously studied, the armor is a type or shadow of a deeper spiritual reality—one that belongs to everyone in Jesus Christ. In order to grasp what the armor is and just what it means to us, we must look beyond the symbols to the spiritual reality. *The armor is a symbolic description of Jesus Christ.* Yes, the armor is Christ. We must learn to appropriate our position in Christ and allow His resurrection life to work itself in us if we yearn for Jesus Christ to be and do everything that He promises in our lives, especially in the midst of this cosmic battle.

It is not uncommon to hear a person proclaim, "Jesus is the answer." While this is certainly true, it is not enough to simply reduce the Christian faith to cheap platitudes and bumper-sticker catchphrases. We must understand the content of what we already believe if we desire truth to impact our lives. Jesus is the answer, amen, but *how* is He the answer? This is what the armor of God teaches. The book of Romans urges us, "Put on the Lord Jesus Christ, and make no provision for the flesh, to gratify its desires" (Romans 13:14). In spiritual warfare the answer *is* Christ—He is our defense—and the armor of God shows us how to appropriate our position in Jesus in times of need.

One last note about the composition of the armor should be pointed out. There is an important distinction made in the six pieces of armor. Each piece falls into either one of two categories. The first three pieces of armor, if anyone is in Christ, have already been done in the past: "*having fastened* on the belt of truth"; "*having put on* the breastplate of righteousness"; "as shoes for your feet, *having put on* the readiness given by the gospel of peace." These things, if you are a believer in Christ, are already yours. They are pieces of armor that have already been put on. You have them on at this very moment, even as you read these words. Consequently, gritting your teeth and trying to be more spiritual won't help you. Likewise, it would silly to ask for any of these things—you currently possess them in Christ.

Conversely, the final three pieces of armor are all things that must be *taken up* in this present moment: "*take up* the shield of faith"; "*take* the helmet of salvation, and the sword of the Spirit." These pieces of armor are our response to all the spiritual blessings we possess in Christ. If we do not take up these three pieces of armor, the first three pieces won't do us much good when we face spiritual attacks.

THE BELT OF TRUTH

The belt of truth is the first piece of armor. "Stand therefore, having fastened on the belt of truth…" (Ephesians 6:14). Soldiers in the ancient Roman army did not wear pants; instead they wore tunics, which came down around their waist like a skirt. Around their tunics each soldier had a belt secured firmly around their waists. Whenever a soldier was about to enter battle, they would first carefully tuck their tunics up under their belts. This would allow their legs to move as freely as possible and allow each soldier to fight unimpeded. Tucking their tunics into their belts showed that each soldier was ready for battle. In the same manner, a Christian "having fastened on the belt of truth" shows that they are prepared. It proves that they are ready for any spiritual attack the enemy may bring. You cannot be ready for battle unless you first have the belt of truth firmly fastened around your waist. Conversely, whenever we feel we are under an attack from the enemy—whether it manifests itself in the form of discouragement, apathy, defeat, even boredom—we should first begin by remembering that we have the belt of truth around us.

What does Jesus being our truth look like? It means that as Christians, we must always remember that in coming to Jesus Christ we have found the ultimate reality, the truth behind all things, the very meaning of life itself. The apostle Paul wrote plainly, "But that is not that way you learned Christ!—assuming that you have heard about him and were taught in him, as truth is in Jesus" (Ephesians 4:20-21). *Truth is in Christ.* In fact, Jesus is the only person in history to boldly claim that He is the only means of salvation, to the exclusion of all other ways, *and* possess the quality of life to back up the claims: "Jesus said to him, 'I am the way, and the truth, and the life. No one comes to the Father except through me.'" (John 14:6). All reality is found in Christ (Colossians 1:17). Every person, every creature, even every object finds its ultimate purpose in the person of Jesus Christ.

I feel in many ways that the church has fallen asleep on things. It is easy to become so caught up in the meaningless affairs of life, the little things that do not matter one bit, only to miss the big picture. I think that as a whole, Christians waste too much time in front of televisions and self-centered hobbies. The days are evil. Instead of redeeming the time, we squander the lean hours of our lives away. In many ways, this is because we have forgotten the belt of truth that we are always wearing. As mortal creatures, we possess what amounts to only a few fleeting moments in a dead and dying world. All men stand guilty and condemned before a holy God, and Jesus

Christ is the only name under heaven by which a man may be saved. Yes, it is the truth that sets one free—and truth is in Christ. We *must* live our lives in light of Jesus as our truth.

THE BREASTPLATE OF RIGHTEOUSNESS

The breastplate of righteousness, the second piece of armor, protects your heart. "Stand therefore, having fastened on the belt of truth, and having put on the breastplate of righteousness..." (Ephesians 6:14). We have discussed the topic of righteous at length, having devoted nearly an entire chapter on it. And yet the importance of our justification can *never* be overemphasized. Just as our Christian life began with justification (purchased by the precious blood of Christ), the blood is always the sole grounds by which we can approach the Lord. Likewise, it is the imputed righteousness of Christ that makes every Christian completely righteous and acceptable to a holy God. Jesus took our place on the cross, having become a curse and condemnation on our behalf, and we have received the full measure of His righteousness. What I'd like to focus in on in this section, however, is how righteousness protects our hearts like a breastplate.

We are as righteous and acceptable to the Lord as Jesus Christ, for the Savior's righteousness has become our own: "For our sake he made him to be sin who knew no sin, so that in him we might become the righteousness of God" (2 Corinthians 5:21). Some of the most precious verses in the Bible to me are the ones that show that in

Christ we have become the very righteousness of God. *Jesus Christ is our righteousness.* This mighty privilege is what the Father has done on our behalf: "He is the source of your life in Christ Jesus, whom God made our wisdom and *righteousness* and sanctification and redemption" (1 Corinthians 1:30). Consequently, what the breastplate of righteousness *really* means is that God is completely satisfied with us in Christ. His wrath has been quenched (as Christ is the propitiation for our sins), and there is no condemnation towards those in Christ (Romans 8:1).

Our righteous standing in Jesus Christ aids us immensely whenever we face spiritual battles. Once we begin to grasp the implications of our justification, we will see just what a privilege each of us has as a child of God. Personally, I always used to feel defeated, guilty, and ashamed, so that I never approached the Lord for help in my time of need. I did not appreciate what my justification provided for me in Christ. What one needs to understand, however, was that because of the blood and righteousness of the Savior, we can *always* approach the Lord for help. It is written in the book of Hebrews:

> Since we then have a great high priest who has passed through the heavens, Jesus, the Son of God, let us hold fast our confession. For we do not have a high priest who is unable to sympathize with our weaknesses, but one who in every respect has been tempted as we are, yet without sin. Let us then with confidence draw near to the throne of grace, that we may receive mercy and find grace to help

in time of need. (Hebrews 4:14-16)

As Christians, we can always approach the Father boldly, in our most desperate hour, and find real help. This is what Christ's blood and righteousness has brought, and this is what the breastplate of righteousness means to every believer.

SHOES OF THE GOSPEL OF PEACE

The third piece of armor that Christians have are "shoes for your feet, having put on readiness given by the gospel of peace" (Ephesians 6:15). It is unthinkable that a soldier would ever take to the battlefield in bare feet. They wouldn't be ready. The rocky terrain would punish the soldier's feet and they would not be able to move freely. In the same manner, a Christian is never ready to face trials or spiritual warfare if they do not first have peace.

The first thing we should notice about peace is that this, once again, is Jesus. *Jesus Christ is our peace.* Jesus is explained in Ephesians, "He himself is our peace" (Ephesians 2:14). This echoes the same words from centuries before, when the Lord spoke of the Messiah through the prophet Micah, "He shall be our peace" (Micah 5:5).

As we have noted before, the order of the armor is crucial. In no other piece of equipment is this seen as in the shoes of peace. One cannot begin with peace, but instead must begin with truth. Jesus Christ is the ultimate reality, the truth behind all things, the only way to God. Only after a Christian has been convinced of that can they then remember who they are in Christ. Every believer, without exception, has become the righteousness of God in Jesus. They are righteous, they are acceptable. And what does all this ultimately lead to? *Peace.* Once one has been justified, they now have peace with a holy God. While before they faced only darkness and condemnation, now justified, a Christian has full, accomplished divine favor. The Scriptures declare, "Therefore, since we have been justified by faith, we have peace with God through our Lord Jesus Christ" (Romans 5:1). So we see that peace only comes through the gospel, and that the peace of God is really peace *with* God.

Some of the last words that Jesus spoke to His disciples were about peace. "Peace I leave with you; my peace I give to you. Not as the world gives do I give to you. Let not your hearts be troubled, neither let them be afraid" (John 14:27). Remember, Jesus gave these words to the disciples at a time that was incredibly difficult and confusing for them. Christ had just told them that He would soon be leaving and they did not understand what He meant. They were as lost orphans in this moment. And yet we can learn from these words, that the Christian can have peace in any circumstance. We can have peace, not only because of the Holy Spirit, the great Comforter, is inside of us, but because the very Prince of Peace Himself has spoken peace to each of our hearts.

We must never fear approaching the Father. We can come boldly into the His presence; with total peace and assurance that He will accept us as a faithful and loving Father wanting to help His children at their time of need. We must not start with trying to gain peace of mind on our own, but must have a peace that is based on the truth that we are righteous and we are loved and accepted by the Lord.

THE SHIELD OF FAITH

We are now moving into the final three pieces of the armor. These three pieces are distinct from the first three, for they each must be *currently* taken up:

> In all circumstances take up the shield of faith, with which you can extinguish all the flaming darts of the evil one; and take up the helmet of salvation, and the sword of the Spirit, which is the word of God. (Ephesians 6:15-16)

The shield of faith is the first of these three pieces of armor that we shall study. I love how faith is described as a shield. But before we dive into the topic, we must begin by remembering that Jesus Christ is "the founder and perfecter of our faith" (Hebrews 12:2). A large portion of the previous chapter was devoted to the topic of faith. Faith is an active trust in what God has promised. Remember, the closest thing we are given to a definition of faith in the Bible is found in the book of Hebrews:

> Now faith is the assurance of things hoped for, the conviction of things not seen. For by it the people of old received their commendation. By faith we understand that the universe was created

260

> by the word of God, so that what is seen
> was not made out of things that are
> visible. (Hebrews 11:1-3)

Immediately following these verses is a lengthy list of many of the Old Testament saints, chronicling all the amazing ways they demonstrated faith. So then, it is crucial to remember that faith is much more than belief. Faith is not only the acceptance of God's word, it is acting upon the word, it is responding to the truth we read in the Bible. But how does faith function as a shield? How does faith protect us from "all the flaming darts of the evil one?" (Ephesians 6:16).

If we examine again the fall in Eden, we see that the first spiritual attack against man was *really* an attack on God's word. The Lord had clearly commanded Adam and Eve not to eat of the tree of the knowledge of good and evil:

> The Lord God took the man and put him
> in the garden of Eden to work it and keep
> it. And the Lord God commanded the
> man, saying, "You may surely eat of every
> tree of the garden, but of the tree of the
> knowledge of good and evil you shall not
> eat, for in the day that you eat of it you
> shall surely die." (Genesis 2:15-17)

God's instructions were clear. However, the devil tried to twist the words of God and undermine the authority of what the Lord had commanded:

> Now the serpent was more crafty than any other beast of the field that the Lord God had made. He said to the woman, "Did God actually say, 'You shall not eat of any tree in the garden'?" And the woman said to the serpent, "We may eat of the fruit of the trees in the garden, but God said, 'You shall not eat of the fruit of the tree that is in the midst of the garden, neither shall you touch it, lest you die.'" But the serpent said to the woman, "You will not surely die. For God knows that when you eat of it your eyes will be opened, and you will be like God, knowing good and evil." (Genesis 3:1-5)

The Lord had spoken one thing and the serpent attacked what God had said. In the same manner, the spiritual attacks that Christians face almost always come in the form of an attack on the authority of Scripture. *Did God really say that? It doesn't really mean what it says, does it?* These assaults are flaming arrows, looking to cast doubts and keep Christians useless in their knowledge of God. And yet our faith can act as a shield.

We need only to contrast the devil's attack in Eden with another spiritual assault—Christ's temptation in the wilderness—if we want to see how faith is a shield. Jesus had spent the previous forty days and nights fasting in the wilderness, and He was very hungry and likely physically weakened from His fast:

> Then Jesus was led up by the Spirit into

> the wilderness to be tempted by the devil.
> And after fasting forty days and forty
> nights, he was hungry. And the tempter
> came and said to him, "If you are the Son
> of God, command these stones to
> become loaves of bread." But He
> answered, "It is written, 'Man shall not
> live by bread alone, but by every word
> that comes from the mouth of God.'"
> (Matthew 4:1-4)

How did Christ respond to the devil's flaming darts? He responded with God's word. Not only did Jesus answer the tempter with Scripture, He stood upon God's word as truth. *He walked by faith in the objective word of God, and His faith worked as a shield, protecting Him from the devil's attack.* Now, a parenthetical note should be placed here: The word of God itself is a different part of the armor, the sword of the Spirit. What I'm looking primarily to here is Christ's faith—the way that He acted upon God's truth. Jesus not only used Scripture as a sword here, He was acting upon it. Christ's response to the word of God is the substance of His faith. God's word and our responding to His word by faith go together like a sword in one hand and a shield in the other. How Jesus Christ responded to the evil one's second temptation was the same:

> Then the devil took him to the holy city
> and set him on the pinnacle of the temple
> and said to him, "If you are the Son of
> God, throw yourself down, for it is
> written, 'He will command His angels

> concerning you,' and 'One their hands
> they will bear you up, lest you strike your
> foot against a stone.'" Jesus said to him,
> "Again it is written, 'You shall not put the
> Lord your God to the test.'" (Matthew
> 4:5-7)

This time the devil tried to directly undermine what the Scripture said by twisting it's meaning around. Christ corrected the lie with the truth—God's truth. And this worked because Jesus was standing firmly upon the truth—He was taking the word's He had read in the Old Testament and united them with faith. The Messiah's final temptation was responded to in a nearly identical manner:

> Again, the devil took him to a very high
> mountain and showed him all the
> kingdoms of the world and their glory.
> And he said to him, "All these things I
> will give you, if you will fall down and
> worship me." Then Jesus said to him,
> "Be gone, Satan! For it is written, 'You
> shall worship the Lord your God and
> Him only shall you serve.'" Then the
> devil left, and behold, angels came and
> were ministering to him. (Matthew 4:8-
> 11)

Christ not only believed the Scripture, He responded to it in faith. His faith was a mighty shield against any attack.

Our faith can help in spiritual warfare as well. But there are a few prerequisites for this. First of all (this should seem obvious), we must know the Bible! We must constantly be studying Scripture, memorizing it, meditating upon it, and ultimately taking the things we read in the Bible and putting them into practice. We must not only know God's truth, we must act upon God's truth. Only then will our faith be thriving and ready for any trials we might face. The connection between exposure to the word of Christ and faith is explained in the book of Romans: "So faith comes by hearing, and hearing thought the word of Christ" (Romans 10:17).

THE HELMET OF SALVATION

The helmet of salvation was the piece of armor that I glazed over the most when I first studied the armor of God several years ago. I did not see the significance in it. But as I've matured in my faith and have become more aware of world events and the trials that people face, I have become impressed more and more by how vital the helmet of salvation is, because it guards the mind of the Christian. It helps us keep an eternal perspective on not only the unfolding world events, but also how we choose to live our daily lives.

The helmet of salvation is really the "helmet of the *hope* of salvation" (1 Thessalonians 5:8). It is the hope of knowing that though darkness and tribulation come our way, or even when we make errors and misstep in our spiritual walk, Christ is working all these things for His good. In fact, the Lord works all events—regardless of how big or small, tragic or otherwise—out for His own glory and the good of those whom He has called. "And we know that for those who love God all things work out for good, for those who are called according to his purpose" (Romans 8:28). The culmination of this working is when Jesus Christ will finally appear to establish His own reign of righteousness and put an end to all evil. That is what the helmet of salvation means. It guards our minds and gives us an eternal perspective. The helmet of the hope of salvation constantly reminds us, "Salvation is nearer to us now than when we first believed" (Romans 13:11).

As I currently write this book, the world is in the midst of a global recession. Countries are in economic turmoil. There have recently been many large scale earthquakes, and floods have devastated entire nations and regions. There is ongoing unrest and constant war in the Middle East. Governments are being overthrown and regimes are changing. These are almost the exact signs Christ spoke of about the final days before His triumphant return:

> "And you will hear of wars and rumors of
> wars. See that you are not alarmed, for
> this must take place, but the end is not
> yet. For nation will rise against nation,
> and kingdom against kingdom, and there
> will be famines and earthquakes in various
> places. All these are but the beginning of
> the birth pains." (Matthew 24:6-8)

These are the signs we see—but the end is not yet. I do not know whether or not we are living in the final days. There is nothing that would mandate that Christ's return occur in the immediate future or even within the next century or millennia. But I am under the personal conviction that things are close. The one thing I know for certain is that every day that passes brings us one day closer to eternity, either by our own deaths or Christ's imminent return. And in the midst of everything, a Christian *always* has hope. No matter what personal trials we may face or world events befall us, we always have hope. In the middle of the darkest black of charcoal night, our hope is as bright and certain as the noon day sun. Christ still reigns! He is still the sovereign Lord over all events of world history. But even much more than that, *Christ is our hope* (1 Timothy 1:1). Taking up the helmet of salvation keeps this blessed hope in the forefront of our minds.

SWORD OF THE SPIRIT

The final piece of the armor that we must take up is the "sword of the Spirit, which is the word of God" (Ephesians 6:17). It should be pointed out that the word of God, just as the other pieces of armor, is Jesus Christ. It is Christ made available to us through His word, in a very real and tangible way. The Bible is essential—it is the only objective and solid means that we know about Jesus Christ and defend orthodoxy. What we first must realize is that the Bible—as the word of God—carries all the authority of the Lord Jesus Christ Himself, for the Bible *is* the word of Christ: "Let the word of Christ dwell in you richly, teaching and admonishing one another in all wisdom, singing psalms and hymns and spiritual songs, with thankfulness in your hearts to God" (Colossians 3:16). The authority of Christ and the authority of the Bible are the same. We cannot separate the two. Consequently, we must submit to the authority of Scripture as much as we would to the very person of Jesus.

What we must see, however, is that while the Bible is the inspired, inerrant word of God, its ultimate purpose is to bear witness to the Son. Christ rightly declared to the Pharisees:

> "And the Father who sent me has himself borne witness about me. His voice you have never heard, his form you have never seen, and you do not have his word abiding in you, for you do not believe the one whom he has sent. You search the Scriptures because you think that in them you have eternal life; and it is they that bear witness about me, yet you refuse to come to me that you may have life."
> (John 5:37-40)

The Pharisees made the foolish mistake of searching the Scriptures yet all the while denying the one whom the Scriptures bore witness of—Jesus Christ. Let us be careful to not make the same error! Every word in the Bible is ultimately there to point men to Jesus, in order that they might repent of their sins and believe in Him for eternal life. Let us make that abundantly clear. If we fail to see this, we risk repeating the folly of Pharisees. The Bible points us to Jesus, to draw near to Him in all situations and all Christ to be our victory. So, the word is a road sign of sorts, pointing us to come to the person of Jesus so that He might give us life.

I hope that you have seen how the armor, instead of merely being a figure of speech or a metaphor, is really the symbol of a deep spiritual reality—the person of Jesus Christ. I firmly believe that God answers all of humanities most fundamental problems, one way or another, in His Son. And yet it is so easy in this age to miss the point. It is so common to have our senses become dulled and distracted. I think in the world today it is far too easy for Christians to lose their footing and slip in their spiritual journey. This is very often the case, at least for me. However, God is not content with leaving His children in apathy and defeat. The Spirit often draws my attention back to true spirituality in Jesus Christ with the same passage in the book of Romans. In fact, it was this passage that I was meditating on when it first became impressed in my mind that the armor *is* Christ:

> Besides this you know the time, that the hour has come for you to wake from sleep. For salvation is nearer to us now than when we first believed. The night is far gone; the day is at hand. So then let us cast off the works of darkness and put on the armor of light. Let us walk properly as in the daytime, not in orgies and drunkenness, not in sexual

> immorality and sensuality, not in quarreling and jealousy. But put on the Lord Jesus Christ, and make no provision for the flesh, to gratify its desires. (Romans 13:11-14)

As I close this book, I want to leave you with one final exhortation. Do not fall asleep. We are in the final age, very close to the last days—if we are not already in them. We must walk properly and not waste the few fleeting moments we have left in our short lives. Jesus pleads with us to come to Him for life. The only things of lasting value find their place ultimately in Christ and bring glory to Him. Will you seek Him? Look away to Jesus and He will be your sufficiency in all things. You will find strength in the midst of weakness. And above all else, whether you face discouragement, trials, or even failures, put these things behind you and press onwards towards the one reality that is before you now—the upward calling of Christ Jesus.

BIBLIOGRAPHY

Austin-Sparks, T. "What is Man?" <u>Spiritual Foundations, Volume 5</u>. Jacksonville: The SeedSowers. 2002.

Boice, James Montgomery. <u>Romans, Volume 2: The Reign of Grace</u>. Grand Rapids: Baker Books. 2008.

Conner, Kevin J. <u>Interpreting the Symbols and Types</u>. Portland: City Bible Publishing. 1992.

George, Bob. <u>Classical Christianity</u>. Eugene: Harvest House. 1989.

---. <u>Complete in Christ</u>. Eugene: Harvest House. 1994.

---. <u>Faith That Pleases God</u>. Eugene: Harvest House. 2001.

Gillham, Bill. <u>Lifetime Guarantee</u>. Eugene: Harvest House. 1993.

Morris, Leon. <u>The Apostolic Preaching of the Cross</u>. Grand Rapids: Eerdmans Printing Company. 2000.

Murray, Andrew. <u>Abiding in Christ</u>. Minneapolis: Bethany House. 2003.

---. <u>The True Vine</u>. New Kensington: Whitaker House. 1982.

---. The Two Covenants. Fort Washington: Christian
    Literature Crusade. 1999.

Nee, Watchman. The Holy Spirit and Reality. Anaheim:
    Living Stream Ministry. 2001.

---. The Normal Christian Life. Wheaton: Tyndale House.
    1977.

---. The Release of the Spirit. New York: Christian
    Fellowship. 2000.

---. Sit, Walk, Stand. Wheaton: Tyndale House. 1977.

---. Christ: The Sum of All Spiritual Things. New York:
    Christian Fellowship. 1973.

Needham, David. Birthright. Sisters: Multnomah. 1999.

Newell, William R. Romans: Verse-by-Verse. Grand
    Rapids: Kregal. 1994.

Owen, John. The Mortification of Sin. San Bernadino.
    2013.

Packer, J.I. Concise Theology. Wheaton: Tyndale House.
    1993.

---. Keep in Step with the Spirit. Grand Rapids: Baker
    Books. 2005.

Piper, John. Counted Righteous in Christ. Wheaton:

Crossway Books. 2002.

Schaeffer, Francis A. <u>The Finished Work of Christ</u>. Wheaton: Crossway Books. 1998.

---. <u>True Spirituality</u>. Wheaton: Tyndale House. 2001.

Solomon, Charles R. <u>Handbook to Happiness</u>. Wheaton: Tyndale House. 1971.

Stanford, Miles J. <u>The Complete Green Letters</u>. Grand Rapids: Zondervan. 1983.

Stedman, Ray C. <u>Authentic Christianity</u>. Grand Rapids: Discovery House. 1996.

---. <u>Hebrews</u>. Downers Grove: InterVarsity Press. 1992.

---. <u>Our Riches in Christ: Discovering the Believer's Inheritance in Ephesians</u>. Grand Rapids: Discovery House. 1998.

---. <u>Spiritual Warfare</u>. Waco: Word Books. 1973.

---. <u>The Way to Wholeness</u>. Grand Rapids: Discovery House. 2005.

Stott, John R.W. <u>Men Made New</u>. Downers Grove: InterVarsity Press. 1977.

Thomas, Major W. Ian. <u>The Indwelling Life of Christ</u>. Sisters: Multnomah Publishers. 2006.

---. <u>The Saving Life of Christ and The Mystery of Godliness</u>. Grand Rapids: Zondervan. 1988.

Towns, Elmer L. <u>The Gospel of John: Believe and Live</u>. Old Tapan: Fleming H. Revell Company. 1990.

Tozer, A.W. <u>The Pursuit of God</u>. Camp Hill: Christian Publications. 1982.

---. <u>The Radical Cross</u>. Camp Hill: Wing Spread Publishers. 2005.

Made in the USA
San Bernardino, CA
30 March 2014